Grade
3

Summer Study
For the Child Going into Third Grade

Written by **Jeanine Manfro**

Illustrations by **Janee Trasler**

FlashKids

New York

FlashKids
New York

An Imprint of Sterling Publishing
387 Park Avenue South
New York, NY 10016

ISBN 978-1-4114-6548-0

Distributed in Canada by Sterling Publishing
c/o Canadian Manda Group, 165 Dufferin Street
Toronto, Ontario, Canada M6K 3H6
Distributed in the United Kingdom by GMC Distribution Services
Castle Place, 166 High Street, Lewes, East Sussex, England BN7 1XU
Distributed in Australia by Capricorn Link (Australia) Pty. Ltd.
P.O. Box 704, Windsor, NSW 2756, Australia

For information about custom editions, special sales, and premium and corporate purchases, please
contact Sterling Special Sales at 800-805-5489 or specialsales@sterlingpublishing.com.

Manufactured in Canada
Lot #:
2 4 6 8 10 9 7 5 3
06/12

www.flashkids.com

Cover design and production by Mada Design, Inc.

DEAR PARENT,

Your child is out of school for the summer, but this doesn't mean that learning has to stop! In fact, reinforcing academic skills in the summer months will help your child succeed during the next school year. This Summer Skills workbook provides activities to keep your child engaged in all the subject areas—Language Arts, Math, Social Studies, and Science—during the summer months. The activities increase in difficulty as the book progresses by reviewing what your child learned in second grade and then introducing skills for third grade. This will help build your child's confidence and help him or her get excited for the new school year!

As you and your child go through the book, look for "Fast Fact" or "On Your Own" features that build upon the theme or activity on each page. At the back of this book you'll find a comprehensive reading list. Keep your child interested in reading by providing some or all of the books on the list for your child to read. You will also find a list of suggested summer projects at the back of this book. These are fun activities for you and your child to complete together. Use all of these special features to continue exploring and learning about different concepts all summer long!

As your child completes the activities in this book, shower him or her with encouragement and praise. You can feel good knowing that you are taking an active and important role in your child's education. Helping your child complete the activities in this book provides him or her with an excellent example—that you value learning, every day! Have a wonderful summer, and most of all, have fun learning together!

TABLE OF CONTENTS

WONDERFUL WATERMELONS

Add the numbers on the slices of watermelon. The first one is done for you.

1. 25 + 36
61

2. 21 + 33
54

3. 56 + 87
133

4. 41 + 59
100

5. 73 + 44
117

6. 82 + 83
165

7. 121 + 232
353

FAST FACT

Have you ever wondered why some watermelon seeds are black and others are white? The black seeds are older than the white ones. As watermelon seeds mature, they change color.

8. 345 + 459
804

9. 654 + 127
781

10. 555 + 350
905

11. 732 + 246
978

12. 403 + 197
600

SCHOOL'S OUT!

Look at the numbers on each bus.
Use the numbers to write four math facts below each bus.

6, 9, 15

6+9=15
9+6=15
15-6=9
15-9=6

4, 7, 11

4+7=11
7+4=11
11-4=7
11-7=

6, 7, 13

6+7=13
7+6=13
13-6=7
13-7=6

5, 4, 9

5+4=9
4+5=9
9-5=4
9-4=5

3, 9, 12

3+9=12
9+3=12
12-3=9
12-9=3

4, 8, 12

4+8=12
8+4=12
12-4=8
12-8=4

8, 9, 17

8+9=17
9+8=17
17-8=9
17-9=8

3, 7, 10

3+7=10
7+3=10
10-3=7
10-7=3

ON YOUR OWN

Make your own math game. Write the numbers 1 to 20 on squares of paper, then place them facedown. Pick up two squares of paper at a time and add them, then put them aside. Continue until there are no squares left.

BUBBLE-BLOWING CONTEST!

Subract the numbers on the bubbles. Circle the bubble with the greatest difference in each row.

17 – 9

8

36 – 27

9

53 – 49

4

86 – 42

44

$$\begin{array}{r} 86 \\ -42 \\ \hline 44 \end{array}$$

73 – 51

22

$$\begin{array}{r} 73- \\ -51 \end{array}$$

69 – 33

36

101 – 43

48

135 – 102

33

247 – 168

79

1317
247 –
– 168
079
+168
247

930 – 642

198

875 – 250

625

444 – 309

135

FAST FACT
The gum that comes with baseball cards is usually covered in a white powder. This powder is powdered sugar. It's used to keep the gum from sticking to other pieces of gum when packages are being put together.

 # FLOWER POWER

Look at the word on each flower. If the word is spelled correctly, color the flower.
Write the correct spellings for the rest of the words in the grass below the flowers.

was

wuz barn said *turn* tirn

black blak *eesy* skurt what

circle right home *square* squair

was
_____
easy
_____
bleak
_____
turn
_____
skirt
_____
square
_____

SUMMER SENTENCES

A sentence is a group of words that tells a complete idea.

For example, this is a sentence:

The sun is shining.

A group of words that does not tell a complete idea is not a sentence.

For example, this is **not** a sentence:

The sun.

Read each group of words. Circle the sentences.

1. We're having a party.

2. Swimming in the pool.

3. Lots of music.

4. Everyone will dance.

5. Swimming races and diving contests.

6. We will serve burgers and chips.

7. We hope you can come.

8. Stamps for the invitations.

ON YOUR OWN

Walk around your house and write down the names of some of the things you see. Then use these words to make sentences. See if you can make these sentences into a story. Read your story to a friend!

Read the groups of words below. Add words to make your own sentences.

9. The bright sun

_____

_____

10. On a hot day

_____

_____

PLANTING A GARDEN

Singular nouns name one person, place, or thing. **Plural nouns** name more than one person, place, or thing. The colored words in the story are nouns. Read the story. Write the singular nouns on the lines on the scarecrow. Write the plural nouns on the clouds.

My family is going to plant a garden. We will grow tomatoes and peppers. First, we will have to dig in the dirt. Then we will plant the seeds. We will pull the weeds and water the plants. We will make a scarecrow to scare away the birds. We will pick the vegetables and wash them in the kitchen. Then my dad will put them in a salad.

Plural Nouns
tomatoes

Singular Nouns

family

ON YOUR OWN
Tomatoes are used in many foods, such as ketchup and spaghetti sauce. Make a list of as many foods as you can that use tomatoes.

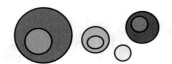 

MAGNET MANIA

Magnets push and pull on certain objects.
They can also push and pull other magnets.

Find out what kinds of objects are attracted to magnets. Find a refrigerator magnet and collect the items in the list below.

crayon   **metal paper clip**
plastic straw   **belt buckle**
scissors   **paper cup**
metal measuring spoon

Hold the magnet next to each item. Write the names of the items that stick to the magnet on the lines below.

1. _____
2. _____
3. _____
4. _____

Lots of people use magnets to stick papers and notes on their refrigerators.
Design a magnet for your refrigerator. Draw a picture of your magnet on the refrigerator below.

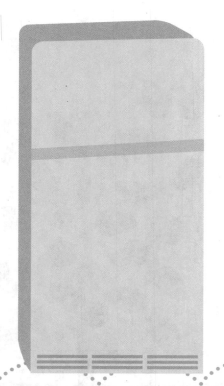

FAST FACT
Earth itself acts like a giant magnet because of gravity. Gravity keeps everything pulled down toward Earth. If you jumped up into the air and there was no gravity, you would go flying off into space instead of landing back on the ground!

A SHIRT FOR DAD

It's Father's Day! Number the sentences in order from **1** to **6** to show the steps involved in getting Dad a shirt for his special day.

_____ The fabric is sent to a factory.

_____ The customer wraps the shirt and gives it to Dad on Father's Day.

_____ The shirt is sold to a store.

_____ Workers at the factory cut and sew the fabric to make the shirt.

_1_ Cotton is grown, harvested, and turned into fabric.

_____ The store sells the shirt to a customer.

Color the shirt below to make a design that you like.

ON YOUR OWN

Make a special scrapbook for your dad for a Father's Day gift. Fill the scrapbook with photographs of the two of you together. Include a letter to your dad thanking him for all that he does for you.

TAKE OFF

Look at the chart to see what time the planes leave the airport.

Flights going to	Leave at
Denver	6:15 AM
New York	7:15 AM
Seattle	10:45 AM
Chicago	12:30 PM
New Orleans	1:30 PM
Los Angeles	2:45 PM

Draw hands on the clocks to show the times the flights leave.

1.

Denver

2.

New York

3.

Seattle

4.

Chicago

5.

New Orleans

6.

Los Angeles

FAST FACT

Brothers Orville and Wilbur Wright invented the first airplane. Wilbur was the first to fly the plane, but the engine failed and he crashed into sand. Luckily, he wasn't hurt. Later, Orville flew the plane for 169 feet. That's about half the length of a football field.

ISLAND SHOPPER

Marcy is going to Hawaii with her family. She wants to buy some souvenirs.
Circle the bills and coins she needs for each gift.

SAILING WITH SYNONYMS

Synonyms are words that mean the same thing. Read the words on the sails. Write a synonym for each word.

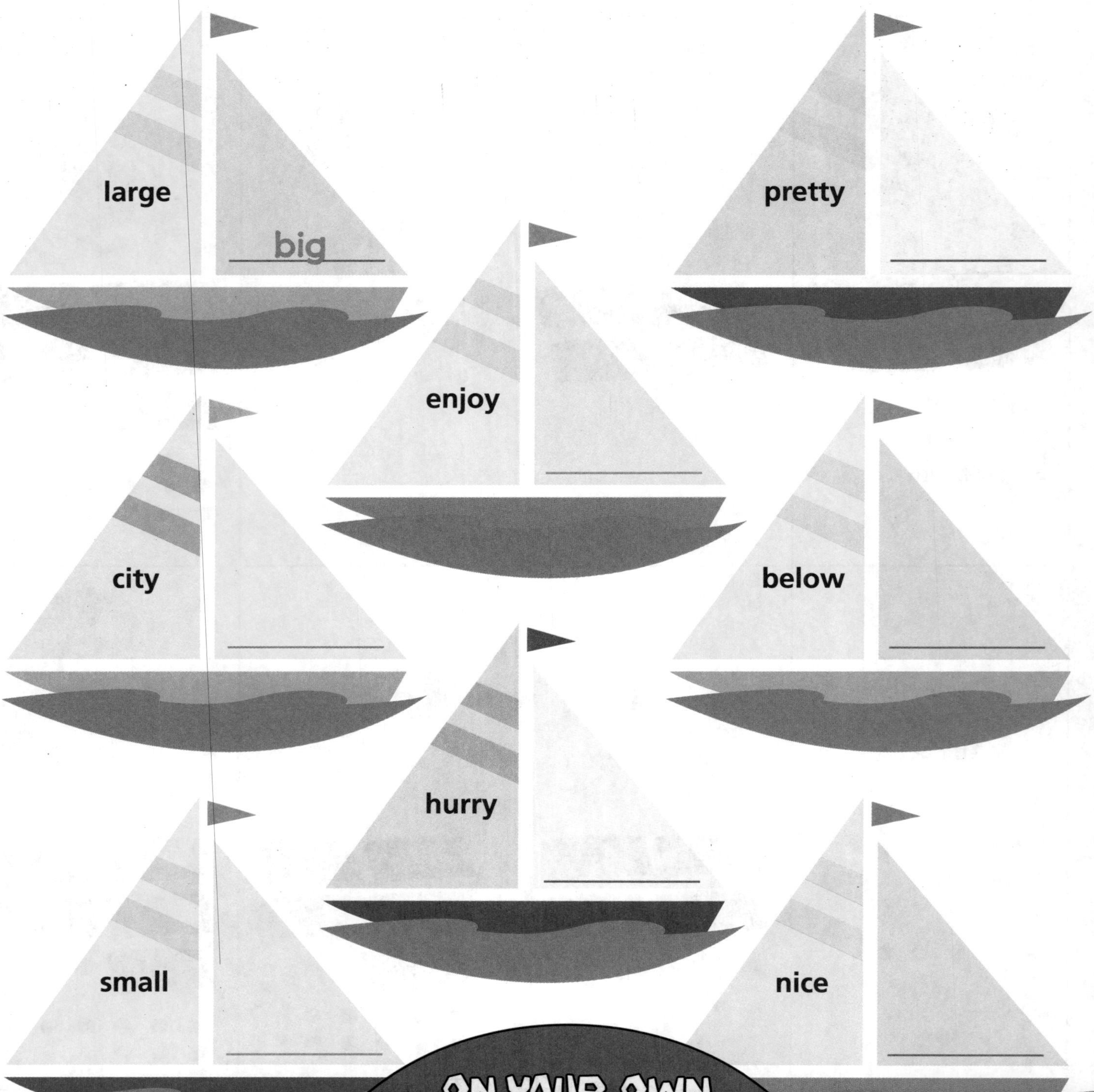

large
big
pretty
enjoy
city
below
hurry
small
nice

ON YOUR OWN

Choose a sentence from one of your favorite books. See if you can rewrite the sentence by using synonyms to change some of the words. For a real challenge, see if you can rewrite all of the sentences on one page of the book.

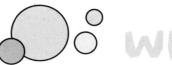 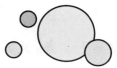

A **prefix** is a small group of letters added to the beginning of a word.
A prefix changes the meaning of the word.

Prefix	Meaning	Example
pre-	before	pre + pay = prepay
un-	not, the opposite	un + pack = unpack
re-	again, back	re + play = replay

Rewrite each sentence. Change the underlined words to words that have the prefixes of
pre-, **un-**, or **re-**.

1. Mom <u>traced</u> our route on the map <u>again</u>.

    Mom retraced our route on the map.

2. The directions to the lake were <u>not clear</u>.

_____

3. Then Dad <u>placed</u> the map <u>back</u> into his backpack.

_____

4. Mom and Dad were <u>not happy</u> about being lost on the trail.

_____

5. "We should have <u>planned</u> our hike <u>before</u>," said Mom.

_____

6. "You're right," said Dad. "We are <u>not prepared</u> for this."

_____

ON YOUR OWN
Make a list of words that begin with the prefixes **pre-**, **un-**, and **re-**. Use each word in a sentence.

SUNNY SAN DIEGO

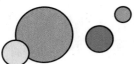
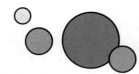

Books have many parts. The **table of contents** is near the beginning of a book.
It tells you the name and page number for each chapter in the book.
A table of contents can help you find information in a book quickly.

This is a table of contents from a book about San Diego, California. Read the table.
Then answer the questions.

1. What chapter tells about hotels?

_____ **Chapter 2** _____

2. What chapter would you read if you wanted to learn what San Diego was like long ago?

_____

3. On what page does Chapter 5 begin?

_____

4. What kind of information would you find in Chapter 3?

_____

5. What begins on page 51?

_____

6. What is the name of the chapter that tells about baseball games?

_____

7. On what page does the index begin?

_____

8. The San Diego Zoo is located in Balboa Park. Which chapter would you read to find out about the zoo?

_____

FAST FACT
L. Frank Baum, the author of *The Wonderful Wizard of Oz*, finished writing some of his books at the beautiful and famous Hotel del Coronado in San Diego.

CRAZY CAVES

Rocks are formed from materials called minerals. Limestone is a type of rock that is made from a mineral. Most caves are made from limestone. Read the journal entry about a trip to the Carlsbad Caverns. Then answer the questions.

June 28

Today we went to the Carlsbad Caverns. This is a whole chain of underground caves. The park ranger told us that the caves started forming millions of years ago. Water seeped through cracks in the limestone rocks and carved out the caves.

Rocks called stalagtites hang down from the roof of the caves. They look like giant icicles. Other rocks, the stalagmites, stick up out of the ground. Tomorrow, we're going to the deepest part of the caverns on the King's Palace tour.

1. What is the name of the caves that the author visited?

The Carlsbad Caverns

2. How long ago did the caves begin to form?

_____

3. What kind of rock are the caves made of?

_____

4. What is the name of a rock formation that hangs down from the roof of a cave?

_____

5. How do you think the author feels visiting the Carlsbad Caverns?

_____

FAST FACT
The Carlsbad Caverns have their very own Bat Cave, home to more than one million bats!

DIG THE DINOS

Dinosaurs lived long ago. Match the picture of the dinosaur to its description.

Apatosaurus
This is a plant-eating dinosaur. It has a very long neck and a tail that can be used like a whip.

Stegosaurus
This is a plant-eating dinosaur. It has spikes on its tail to use as a weapon. It has plates on its back for protection.

Tyrannosaurus rex
This is a meat-eating dinosaur. It is very large, but it has small arms.

Triceratops
This is a plant-eating dinosaur. It has three horns on its head.

Compsognathus
This is a meat-eating dinosaur. It is about the size of a chicken.

FAST FACT
The Sauroposeidon is thought to have been the largest dinosaur. It was about 60 feet tall!

IN THE AIR WITH AMELIA

Read the story. Then answer the questions.

Amelia Earhart was born on July 24, 1897. She was different from other girls her age. She enjoyed climbing trees and playing baseball. She rode horses, went fishing, and caught frogs and toads. She even helped build a roller coaster in her grandparents' yard. Amelia was smart and brave. When she grew up, she became one of the first female pilots. She was the first woman to ever fly alone across the Atlantic Ocean, but she had an even bigger dream. Amelia wanted to fly all the way around the world along the equator. No one, man or woman, had ever done that before. Amelia set out to follow her dream. Sadly though, her plane was lost near the end of her journey. No one knows for sure what happened to Amelia, but most people think that her plane crashed into the ocean. Amelia Earhart's bravery still inspires people today.

Circle the sentences below that are **true**.
Cross out the sentences that are **false**.

1. Amelia helped build a roller coaster.

2. Amelia Earhart liked to sit quietly.

3. Amelia flew airplanes.

4. Amelia drove a car across the Atlantic Ocean.

5. Amelia wanted to fly around the globe.

6. People think that Amelia's plane crashed.

FAST FACT
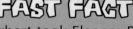
Amelia Earhart took Eleanor Roosevelt on a flight over Washington, D.C. Mrs. Roosevelt was the First Lady at the time and had planned to take flying lessons from Amelia.

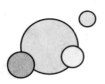
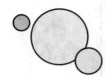

CAMP SUMMERLAND

Welcome to Camp Summerland! Compare the numbers on each canoe.
Write <, >, or = in the circles.

1. 34 < 43

2. 13 ◯ 31

3. 16 ◯ 27

4. 25 ◯ 35

5. 451 ◯ 154

6. 1,000 ◯ 999

7. 333 ◯ 343

8. 987 ◯ 789

9. 24 ◯ 11 + 13

10. 300 ◯ 200 + 200

11. 53 ◯ 5 + 30

12. 500 ◯ 250 + 25

PIZZA PARTY

It's Pizza Night at Camp Summerland. If all the campers living in one cabin will get the same amount of pizza, how many pieces of pizza does each camper get?

1. The Antelope Cabin has 6 campers.
Each camper will get ___2___ pieces of pizza.

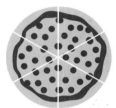 

2. The Bobcat Cabin has 8 campers.
Each camper will get _____ pieces of pizza.

 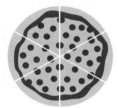 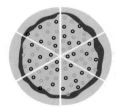 

3. The Cheetah Cabin has 5 campers.
Each camper will get _____ pieces of pizza.

4. The Donkey Cabin has 4 campers.
Each camper will get _____ pieces of pizza.

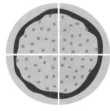 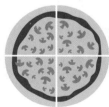 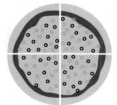

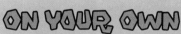

ON YOUR OWN
The next time you eat pizza, try to figure out what fraction of a pizza pie you ate.

5. In which cabin do the campers get the fewest slices of pizza?

_____

6. In which two cabins do the campers get the same number of slices of pizza?

_____

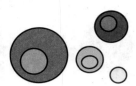

PLAYFUL PATTERNS

The Summerland Campers are stringing beads to make necklaces.
Help them finish the necklaces. Fill in the missing numbers.

1. 5 7 9 11 13 15 17 19

2. 2 4 8 ___ ___ 64 ___ ___

3. 4 8 ___ ___ 20 24 ___ ___

4. 35 ___ 45 50 ___ 60 65 70

5. 150 200 ___ 300 350 ___ ___ 500

6. 90 ___ 70 ___ 50 ___ 30 20

7. ___ 21 18 ___ 12 9 ___ 3

8. 410 400 ___ 380 ___ 360 ___ 340

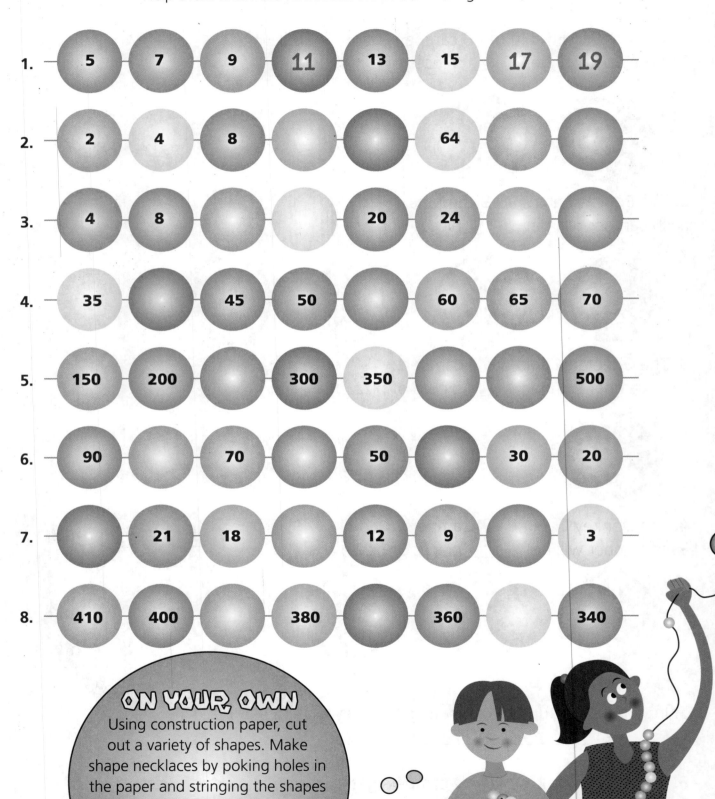

ON YOUR OWN

Using construction paper, cut out a variety of shapes. Make shape necklaces by poking holes in the paper and stringing the shapes onto pieces of yarn. How many different patterns can you come up with for your necklaces?

SPLISH, SPLASH!

Antonyms are words that have opposite meanings.
Circle the antonym for the underlined word in each sentence.

1. It was a <u>warm</u> day at Camp Summerland.   (cool)   clear

2. The children <u>ran</u> to the pool.   **skated**   **walked**

3. Justin climbed the ladder for the <u>high</u> dive.   **sky**   **low**

4. When he jumped into the water, he made a <u>loud</u> splash.   **quiet**   **wide**

5. Soon, there were <u>many</u> children swimming in the pool.   **few**   **several**

Read the words below. Write an antonym for each one.

6. soft _____   **7.** first _____

8. wide _____   **9.** left _____

10. different _____   **11.** happy _____

ON YOUR OWN

Make a set of flashcards with antonym pairs. Use them to play a game of charades with a friend. Choose a flashcard and act out the first word. See if your friend can guess the antonyms.

DEAR FRIEND

Write a letter to a friend telling him or her all about your summer.

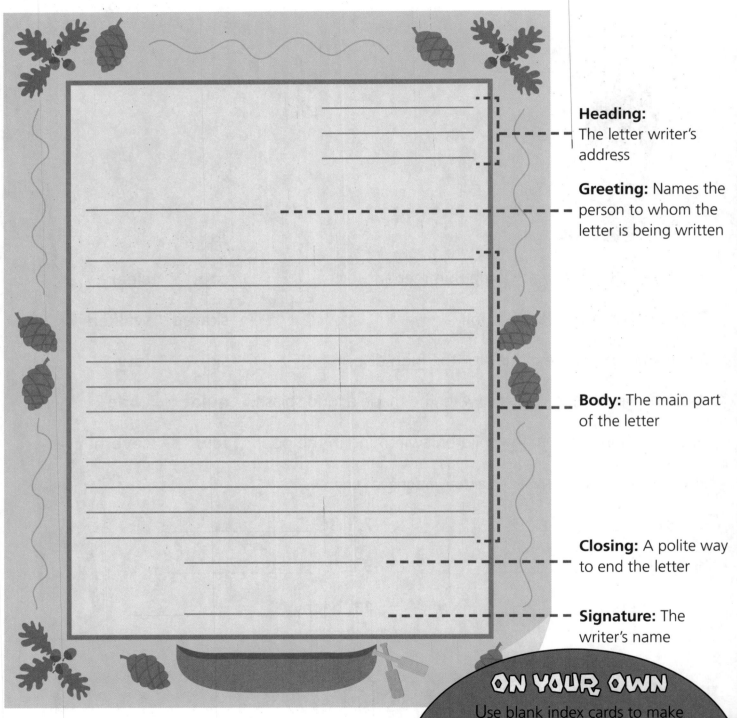

Heading: The letter writer's address

Greeting: Names the person to whom the letter is being written

Body: The main part of the letter

Closing: A polite way to end the letter

Signature: The writer's name

ON YOUR OWN

Use blank index cards to make postcards. On one side of each index card, draw a picture. On the other side, write a short letter or message to a friend or family member. Be sure to put stamps and addresses on the postcards before you mail them.

THE CIRCLE OF LIFE

Number the sentences from **1** to **5** to show the life cycle of a butterfly and a frog.

_____ Inside the chrysalis, the caterpillar's body begins to change.

_____ When the chrysalis opens up, a butterfly comes out.

_____ The caterpillar hangs itself from a twig and forms a chrysalis.

__1__ A caterpillar hatches from an egg.

_____ As the caterpillar eats and grows, it sheds its skin.

_____ A frog egg is laid in water.

_____ When the tail is completely gone, it has turned into a frog.

_____ A tadpole begins to form inside the egg.

_____ The tail starts to shrink and legs begin to grow.

_____ The tadpole hatches from the egg with a tail and no legs.

FAST FACT
Have you ever felt silk? Silk is made from the threads that some caterpillars use to spin their cocoons. These threads are spun into smooth, soft fabric.

Look at the map. Then answer the questions.

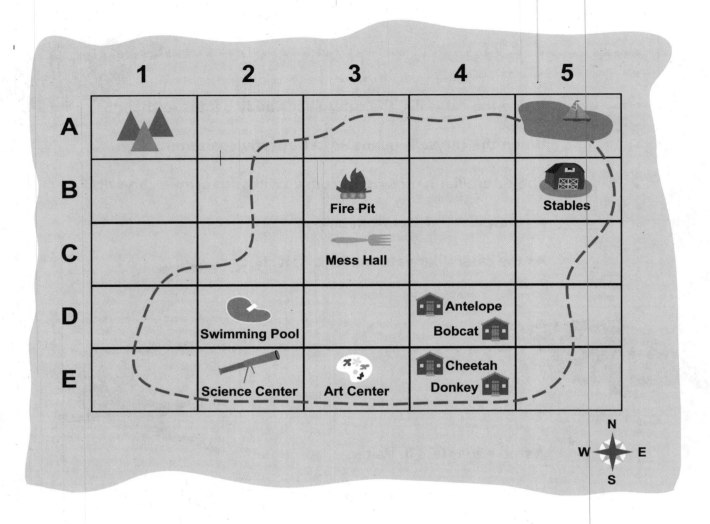

1. Write the grid coordinates for the location of the fire pit. **B3**

2. In what direction would you travel to get from the art center to the fire pit?

_____

3. Write the gird coordinates for the location where the hiking trail begins and ends. _____

4. In which directions would you have to travel to get from the cabins to the lake? _____

5. What is directly south of the lake?

_____

6. What is directly east of the science center?

_____

HELLO, DADDY-O!

At Camp Summerland, grandparents are invited to visit for a day.
The campers decorate the camp to look like the 1950s, the time when many of their grandparents were kids. Read the story about Grandparent's Day. Then answer the questions.

On Grandparent's Day, it feels like we're going back in time. All the girls at Camp Summerland wear poodle skirts and blouses. The boys wear cowboy shirts and ties. We invite our grandparents to join us in hula hoop contests. After dinner, we hold a sock hop. I make sure that my grandpa's name is the first and last one on my dance card. Learning about the 1950s is fun!

Use words from the story to finish the sentences.

1. In the 1950s, many girls wore ___poodle skirts and blouses___ .

2. _____ and _____ were popular clothes for boys.

3. There were contests to see how long people could spin a _____ around their bodies.

4. At a _____ , people danced in their socks.

5. _____ were used to tell who you would dance with during each song.

FAST FACT
Elvis Presley recorded his first two songs in 1953. He became so popular that people called him the King of Rock and Roll.

BATTER UP!

Draw a picture, chart, or diagram to solve the story problems.
Then write the answer for each problem.

1. Kate, Marco, and Jenna are lining up for batting practice. How many different ways can they line up?
___6___

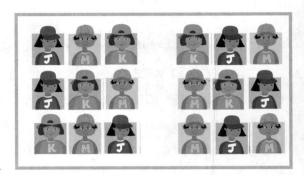

2. Kate hit 16 balls on Monday, 22 balls on Wednesday, and 15 balls on Friday. How many balls did she hit in all?

_____

3. Jenna practices batting for 30 minutes a day, three days a week. How many weeks will it take her to practice for a total of 6 hours?

_____

4. Marco hit his first ball 12 feet. He hit the second ball 14 feet, and the third ball 16 feet. If he continues in this pattern, how far will he hit the tenth ball?

_____

FAST FACT

In 2001, a new kind of bat hit the shelves at toy stores. The JD Batball is a hollow plastic bat that can be used to store baseballs. It was invented by a six-year-old boy so that he would never forget to bring baseballs along with his bat!

SUPERSONIC SLUGGERS

The Supersonic Sluggers played eight baseball games.
The graph shows the number of runs scored in each game.

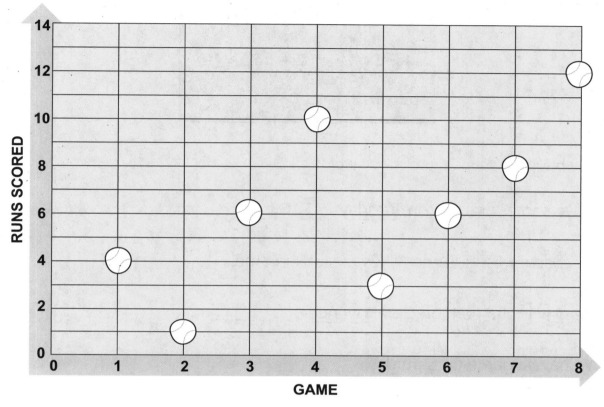

Use the graph to answer the questions.

1. How many runs did the team score in Game 2? __1__

2. In which two games did the team score the same number of runs? _____

3. What is the difference between the team's highest score and its lowest score? _____

4. What is the total number of runs scored in Games 5, 6, and 7? _____

ON YOUR OWN
Keep track of your favorite baseball team's scores. Make a graph and mark the team's score after every game. Can you tell if the team plays better in its home stadium or in other stadiums?

 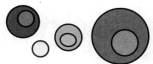

SHORTEN IT

An **abbreviation** is a shorter way of writing a word.
Abbreviations start with capital letters and end with periods.

> **Ash Street** becomes **Ash St.**
>
> **Monday** becomes **Mon.**
>
> **Doctor** becomes **Dr.**

Write the abbreviation for each underlined word.

1. I have soccer practice on Tuesday. **Tues.**

2. My coach, Missus Turner, likes to start on time. _____

3. We play in the park on Coral Avenue. _____

4. We have a game on Saturday. _____

5. We'll be playing the Texas Tornadoes on Wednesday. _____

6. Afterward, we'll go to the pizza parlor on Cactus Drive. _____

7. My neighbor, Doctor Bates, always buys the pizzas for my team. _____

8. The season will be over in August. _____

FAST FACT
Every four years, the biggest soccer tournament in the world is played. It is called the World Cup. Billions of people around the world watch the games on television.

GOAL!

A **noun** is a person, place, or thing. A **verb** tells what a person or thing is doing.
An **adjective** describes a noun.

Read the words on the soccer balls. If the word is a **noun**, color the ball orange. If the word is a **verb**, color the ball purple. If the word is an **adjective**, color the ball green.

game kick hard

ball quick jump

run net happy

GRANDPA'S PROMISE

Read the story. Then answer the questions.

Casey's sandals slapped at the bottoms of her feet as she raced along. Today was a special day. Grandpa was visiting and he had made a promise. Grandpa unlocked the gate to the swimming pool. Casey ran inside and dropped her towel on one of the plastic chairs. "Now, Grandpa? Can you show me now?" she begged.

Grandpa chuckled. "Just a minute. I've got to put my glasses on first." Finally, Grandpa joined Casey by the side of the pool. "Now, put your toes right there by the edge."

Suddenly, Casey was nervous. She wondered, "What if I land on my belly? What if I crash my head against the bottom?"

Grandpa stood right beside her. "Reach your arms up over your head, like you're going to touch the sky. Then bend over like you're going to touch your toes." Grandpa watched carefully. "Ready? Go!"

Casey tipped over the side of the pool. Her fingers touched the water first, and then her body followed. She had learned to dive!

1. What had Grandpa promised Casey? ___Grandpa promised to___ ___teach Casey how to dive.___

2. How did Casey feel at the beginning of the story? _____
_____

3. Why did Casey start to feel nervous? _____
_____

4. How do you think Casey felt at the end of the story? _____
_____

5. What word in the story means the same thing as **laughed**? _____
_____

Motion is what happens when something moves from where it was to a new place.
Force is what causes an object to move. The object is pushed or pulled by force.
Speed is how fast an object moves. **Friction** causes an object to stop moving.

Read each sentence. If the sentence is **true**, color the bat. If the sentence is **false**, cross out the bat.

1. When you throw a ball, you are using force to make it move.

2. It is not possible to measure the speed of a moving object.

3. Kicking a soccer ball changes the position of the ball.

4. A rolling ball can only stop if someone picks it up.

5. The harder you kick a ball, the slower it will move.

6. Friction from water slows down swimmers.

ON YOUR OWN

Place a table tennis ball in the middle of a table. Stand on one side of the table and ask a friend to stand on the other side. At the same time, both of you will try to blow the ball off the table. Who can blow with the strongest force?

A LITTLE HELP

Machines are tools used to move objects.
Machines help people use force to push or pull things. A bowling ball is a machine.
When it is rolled down a bowling alley, it pushes the bowling pins down.

Circle the pictures of objects that are machines.

FAST FACT

A surfboard is a machine that helps people move through the water. Surfing was invented by Hawaiians hundreds of years ago. It was a popular sport even among the kings and queens of the islands.

Many people play sports during the summer. Using **good sportsmanship** means that players behave well during the game. They play fairly, show respect to others, and are kind whether they win or lose.

Write a sentence on each medal that tells one thing about good sportsmanship.

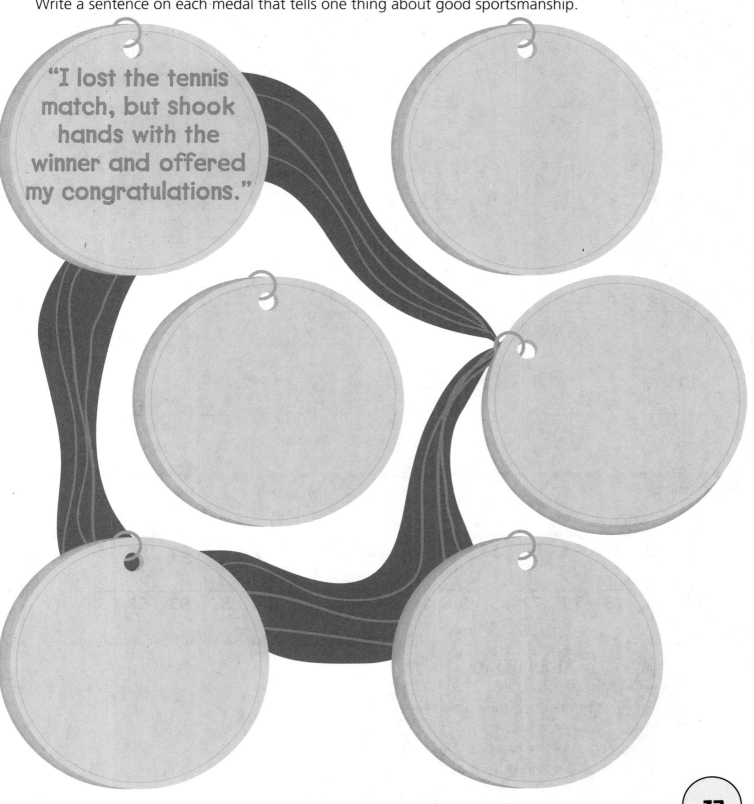

"I lost the tennis match, but shook hands with the winner and offered my congratulations."

GOOD QUESTION

Why do elephants have trunks?

Solve the problems. Use subtraction to check your answers.
Then use the letters next to the sums to fill in the answer to the riddle.

1. 45
        + 53   E   98
        —————   - 45
        98   ————
                         53

2. 26   T   -____
        + 34
        ————

3. 75   C   -____
        + 12
        ————

4. 18   B   -____
        + 39
        ————

5. 69   A   -____
        + 24
        ————

6. 35   U   -____
        + 15
        ————

7. 47   R   -____
        + 28
        ————

8. 29   S   -____
        + 29
        ————

9. 61   H   -____
        + 24
        ————

10. 17   N   -____
        + 39
        ————

11. 63   I   -____
        + 32
        ————

12. 55   Y   -____
        + 17
        ————

Answer:

| 57 | 98 | 87 | 93 | 50 | 58 | 98 | | 60 | 85 | 98 | 72 | | 87 | 93 | 56 | 60 |

| 87 | 93 | 75 | 75 | 72 | | 93 | | 58 | 50 | 95 | 60 | 87 | 93 | 58 | 98 |

FAST FACT

Can you use your nose to drink?
An elephant can! Its trunk is actually
a very long nose and an upper lip.
When an elephant wants a drink, it
sucks up about two gallons of water
into its trunk. Then it brings its
trunk up and blows the water into
its mouth.

SWINGING SUBTRACTION

Subtract. Regroup when you need to.

1.
```
   3 1
  7̶4̶3̶
- 225
  518
```

2.
```
  321
- 211
```

3.
```
  549
- 269
```

4.
```
  936
- 777
```

5.
```
  148
-  57
```

6.
```
  250
- 109
```

7.
```
  464
- 132
```

8.
```
  659
- 269
```

9.
```
  851
- 664
```

10.
```
  638
- 229
```

FAST FACT
Chimpanzees spend most of their time in trees. When they do walk on the ground, they use their knuckles for support.

BIRDS OF A FEATHER

A zookeeper takes care of her zoo's birds.
She made a bar graph to show the number of birds that are in her care. Look at the graph.
Then answer the questions.

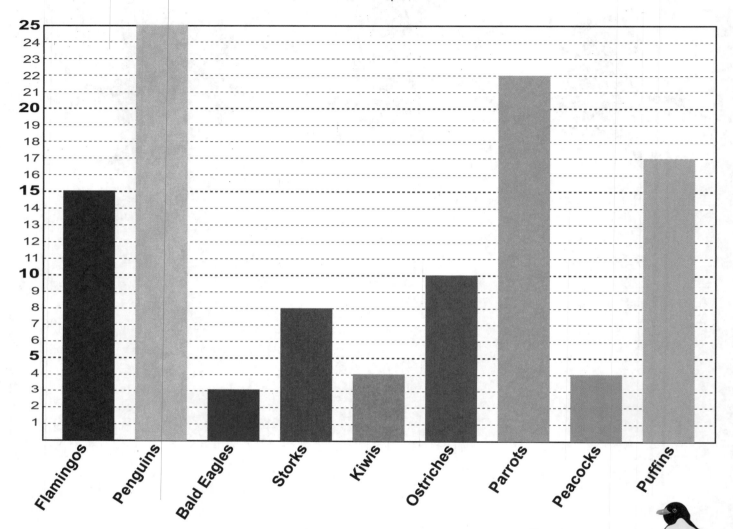

1. How many bald eagles does the zookeeper care for? ___3___

2. How many birds, all together, does the zookeeper care for? _____

3. How many more penguins are there than puffins? _____

4. How many more parrots are there than storks? _____

5. There is an equal number of which two types of birds? _____

_____

6. Which of the following is **not** found in the graph? _____
   a) the difference between the number of flamingos and
      the number of storks at the zoo
   b) what countries the birds are native to
   c) how many ostriches the zookeeper takes care of

FAST FACT
Have you ever heard the saying "You are what you eat"? For flamingos, that is especially true. They get their pink color from the shrimp they eat.

A TRIP TO THE ZOO

Sentences can be written in many different ways to make them more interesting.
They can begin with different words. They can be different lengths.
Two sentences can be combined to make one sentence.

Read each set of sentences. Rewrite them to make them more interesting.

1. My brother went to the zoo. I went with him.

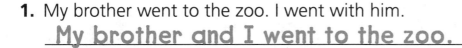

  My brother and I went to the zoo.

2. We saw lions. We saw tigers. We saw bears.

_____

_____

3. I liked the tigers the best. My brother liked the bears better.

_____

_____

4. After lunch, we went to see the monkeys. After lunch, we went to see the polar bears.

_____

_____

5. We shopped at the gift shop before we left. I bought a T-shirt. My brother bought a T-shirt.

_____

_____

6. I was sad to leave the zoo. I wanted to stay longer.

_____

_____

ON YOUR OWN
Write a story about a trip you took with someone in your family. Include lots of details of what you saw and how you felt.

SUPER SENTENCES

A sentence can end with a **period** (.), a **question mark** (?),
or an **exclamation point** (!).

A **period** is used after a statement or a command.
A **question mark** is used after a question.
An **exclamation point** is used to show excitement. It follows an exclamation.

Use a **period,** a **question mark,** or an **exclamation point** to finish each sentence.

1. What a great day we had __!__

2. We went to the zoo and learned all about the animals ____

3. Did you know that lions walk on their tiptoes ____

4. Can you guess what a rhino uses its horns for ____

5. We looked at the giraffes ____

6. I can't believe how many amazing animals there are ____

FAST FACT
Rhinos use their horns as weapons. Males use them in fights with other animals and females use them to protect their young from predators.

Now practice writing your own sentences.
Write at least one statement, one question, and one exclamation.

_____

_____

_____

_____

_____

_____

ENDANGERED SPECIES

An **endangered species** of animals is one that is in danger of becoming extinct, or dying out.
Many animals are endangered. Color the pictures below of endangered animals.
Then write whether the animal is a **mammal**, **bird**, or **fish**.

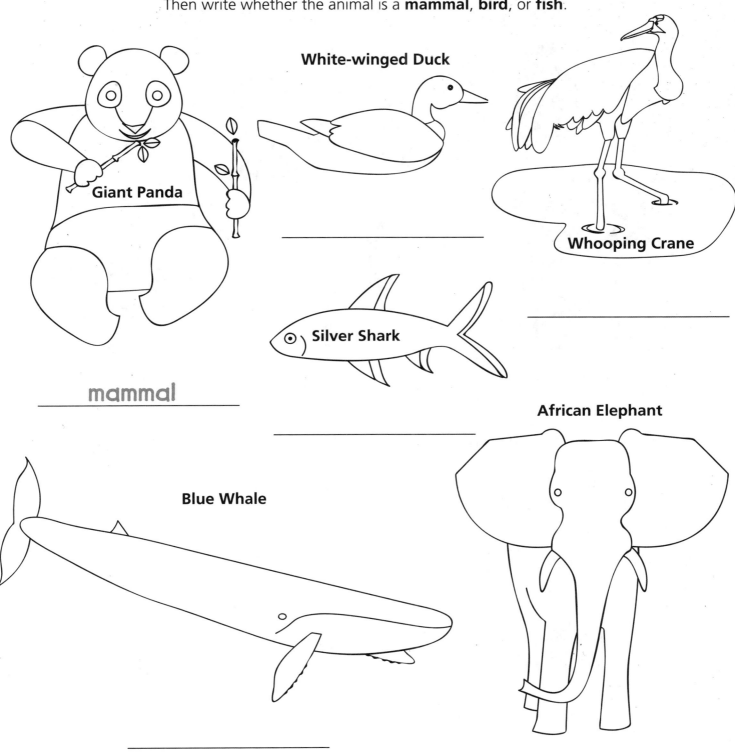

White-winged Duck

Giant Panda

Whooping Crane

Silver Shark

mammal

African Elephant

Blue Whale

Look at the zoo map. Then answer the questions

1. In which direction would you walk to go from the elephants to the gorillas?

   Northwest

2. What is directly south of the reptiles?

   _____

3. What is northwest of the giraffes?

   _____

4. Write directions telling someone how to get from the gorillas to the giraffes, and then to the elephants.

   _____

   _____

   _____

ON YOUR OWN
Draw a map of your community. Use the map to write directions from your house to your school.

THE U.S. GOVERNMENT

Fill in the blanks with words from the word box.

White House	**Liberty Bell**	**constitution**
"The Star-Spangled Banner"	**flag**	**Statue of Liberty**

1. Our Founding Fathers wrote the _____ constitution _____.

2. The president of the United States lives in the _____.

3. The _____ is a symbol of freedom. It cracked after arriving in the United States.

4. _____ was written by Francis Scott Key in 1814.

5. New stars are added to the _____ each time a new state joins the union.

6. Now located in New York, the _____ was a gift from France.

FAST FACT
George Washington was the first president of the United States. He helped to create our nation!

45

FARM FOOD

Use the pictures to help you solve the problems.

4 + 4 + 4

1. 3 x 4 = ___12___

7 + 7 + 7 + 7 + 7

2. 5 x 7 = _____

12 + 12 + 12 + 12

3. 4 x 12 = _____

3 + 3 + 3 + 3 + 3 + 3 + 3 + 3 + 3

4. 9 x 3 = _____

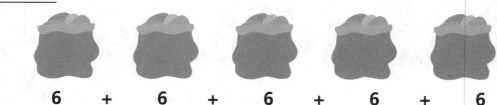

6 + 6 + 6 + 6 + 6

5. 5 x 6 = _____

ANIMAL PENS

The farmer is building pens for his animals.
Use the word problems to help you solve the division problems.

1. There are 10 horses on the farm. Each pen can hold 5 horses. How many pens are needed?

$10 \div 5 =$ ___2___

2. There are 24 pigs on the farm. Each pen can hold 8 pigs. How many pens are needed?

$24 \div 8 =$ _____

3. There are 36 cows on the farm. Each pen can hold 4 cows. How many pens are needed?

$36 \div 4 =$ _____

4. There are 48 chickens on the farm. Each pen can hold 6 chickens. How many pens are needed?

$48 \div 6 =$ _____

5. There are 27 sheep on the farm. Each pen can hold 9 sheep. How many pens are needed?

$27 \div 9 =$ _____

6. There are 33 goats on the farm. Each pen can hold 3 goats. How many pens are needed?

$33 \div 3 =$ _____

MATCH UP!

A **compound word** is made up of two or more words that are joined together to make a new word. Match the words to make compound words. Write the compound words.

1. _____farmhouse_____
2. _____
3. _____
4. _____
5. _____
6. _____
7. _____
8. _____

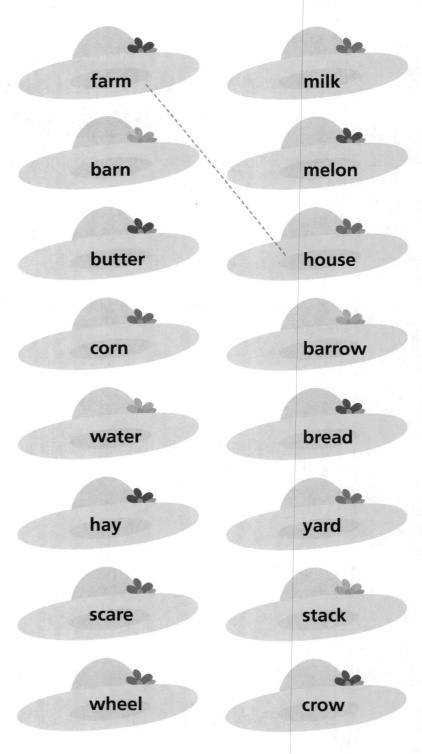

farm

milk

barn

melon

butter

house

corn

barrow

water

bread

hay

yard

scare

stack

wheel

crow

ON YOUR OWN

Play a memory match game. Make a list of compound words. On separate index cards, draw a picture of each word in the compound. Mix up the cards and place them facedown in rows. Turn two cards over at a time to try to find a match. The game is over when all of the matches have been made.

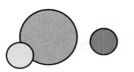
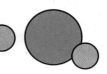

Read the story. Then rewrite the story using the correct capitalization.

in july, becky and jim visited aunt tonya's farm. on their first day there, they swam in sunstone creek. afterward, they hiked up butler's hill. the next day they collected eggs! aunt tonya said they could sell the eggs at the farmers' market on main street. on saturday, they helped clean the horse stalls before their riding lessons. that evening, aunt tonya took everyone on a hayride. becky and jim had a great time on the farm.

_____

_____

_____

_____

_____

_____

_____

_____

_____

ON YOUR OWN

Write a story about a day on a farm. Tell about all of the sights, sounds, and smells you would experience during your visit.

DID YOU KNOW?

Read the story. Then answer the questions.

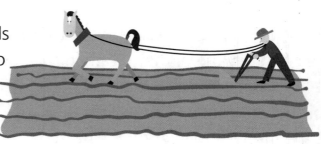

Farming is a very old trade. It began thousands of years ago when people first learned how to grow crops and raise animals. Early farmers shared fields. But over time, they began to fence off their own portions of the fields.

They also learned to rotate the crops that they planted. For example, if a farmer planted a field with wheat one year, the next year he might plant turnips. This helps keep the soil fresh and full of nutrients. About 200 years ago, people started to invent machines to make farming easier. Now, more food can be produced with less work. Today, about half of the world's people are farmers. Some farmers grow just enough food to feed themselves. Others grow cash crops, or food that is produced to be sold.

1. What is this story about?
a) what life on a farm is like
b) the history of farming
c) a farm animal's adventures
d) the world's most common crops

2. When did farming begin?
a) thousands of years ago
b) 200 years ago
c) one year ago
d) in the 1600s

3. Why is crop rotation a good practice?
a) It gives the farmers more things to eat.
b) It makes farming easier.
c) More crops can be grown.
d) It helps keep the soil fresh and full of nutrients.

4. About how many of the world's people are farmers?

a) $\frac{2}{3}$ b) $\frac{1}{2}$

c) $\frac{1}{4}$ d) $\frac{5}{6}$

5. What is a cash crop?
a) a grove of money trees
b) a crop that is sold
c) a crop that is traded for other goods
d) food that is grown just to feed the farmer

FAST FACT
Rice is one of the most important crops in the world. It grows best in warm, moist climates.

Use the words in the box to label the parts of this strawberry plant.

flowers	leaves
fruit	roots

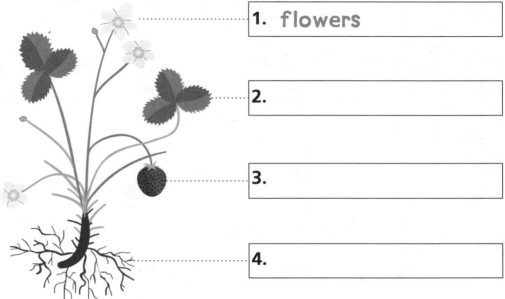

1. flowers

2. _____

3. _____

4. _____

Use the words in the box to finish the sentences.

roots	nutrients	water
air	seeds	sunlight

5. Plants get _____ and _____ from soil.

6. The plants use water, _____ , and _____ to make food.

7. The _____ grow underground and hold a plant in place.

8. Tiny plants grow inside of _____ .

ON YOUR OWN
Find out what's inside a seed! Soak a bean seed in a cup of water overnight. In the morning, pull off the seed's skin and split the seed in half lengthwise. Draw a picture of what you see inside.

WATCH US GROW

Plants and animals need many things to grow.
In the first row of boxes, draw pictures of things that plants need.
In the second row, draw pictures of things that animals need.

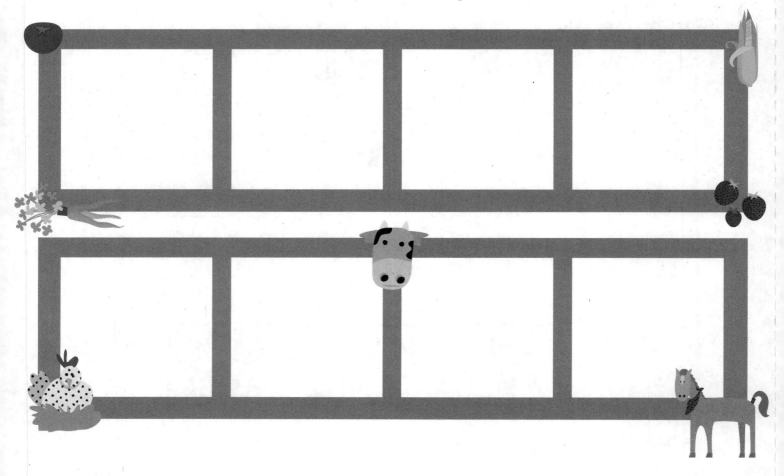

Write a few sentences that tell about the things that plants and animals need.

ON YOUR OWN

Make a chart that shows the things you need in order to grow up strong and healthy. Circle the things that plants and animals need too.

_____

_____

_____

_____

_____

_____

_____

BUSINESS AS USUAL

Farms are businesses. They provide food that people need.
Choose the answer for each question below.

1. John and Maya have a business. They clean out the animal pens at farms in their town. Which of these statements is true about their business?
    a) John and Maya make things to sell.
    b) John and Maya sell things for other people.
    c) John and Maya provide a service.

2. Which of the following is the most likely to cause the cost of corn to go up?
    a) A storm damages many crops.
    b) Farm workers earn less money.
    c) The price of tomatoes goes down.

3. Brenda says she will repair one of Tom's fences if he will paint her barn. Which of these statements is true about Brenda and Tom?
    a) They will not get money for the work they do for each other.
    b) Brenda will be paid for her work.
    c) Tom will sell Brenda's barn.

4. For lunch, Brianna is having a peanut butter sandwich, an apple, a cookie, and milk. Which statement is probably true?
    a) Brianna's family owns a farm and made all of the items in her lunch.
    b) Brianna's family went to a farm and traded things for the items in her lunch.
    c) The items in Brianna's lunch were bought at a store. The store bought the items from many different businesses.

5. A dairy farm is the largest business in a small town. Which statement is probably true?
    a) The farm provides many jobs for the people in the town.
    b) The farm sells fruits and vegetables to the people in the town.
    c) The farm pays for the people's houses.

SKIPPING UP THE MOUNTAIN

Start at the bottom of each mountain. Skip count your way to the top.

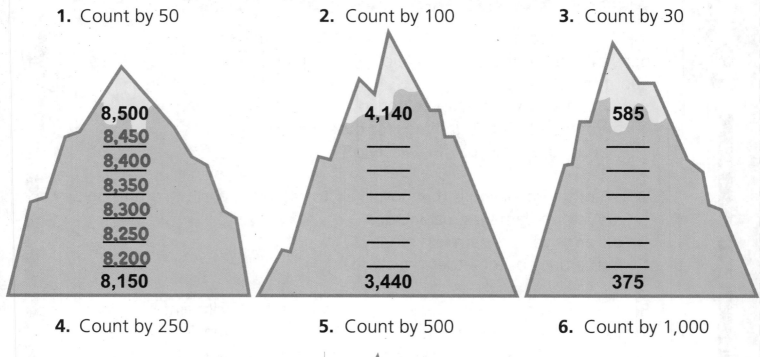

1. Count by 50

8,500
8,450
8,400
8,350
8,300
8,250
8,200
8,150

2. Count by 100

4,140
____
____
____
____
____
____
3,440

3. Count by 30

585
____
____
____
____
____
____
375

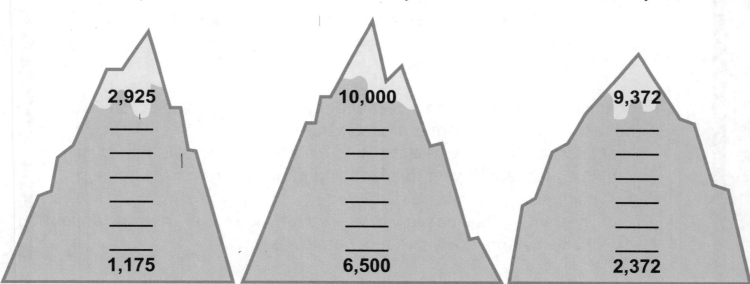

4. Count by 250

2,925
____
____
____
____
____
1,175

5. Count by 500

10,000
____
____
____
____
____
6,500

6. Count by 1,000

9,372
____
____
____
____
____
2,372

TENT TIME

Write the number shown on each tent in expanded form.

1. 1,265

_1,000_ + _200_ + _60_ + _5_

2. 6,732

_____ + ____ + ____ + ____

3. 8,388

_____ + ____ + ____ + ____

4. 3,954

_____ + ____ + ____ + ____

5. 2,542

_____ + ____ + ____ + ____

6. 4,320

_____ + ____ + ____ + ____

7. 5,555

_____ + ____ + ____ + ____

8. 7,021

_____ + ____ + ____ + ____

ON YOUR OWN

Ask your family and friends if they have ever been camping. If so, ask what was their favorite part. Make a graph of the answers.

TOASTING MARSHMALLOWS

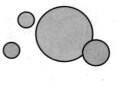

Round the numbers on these marshmallows to the nearest 10.

1. 54 — 50

2. 68 — _____

3. 127 — _____

4. 2,321 — _____

Round the numbers on these marshmallows to the nearest 100.

5. 891 — 900

6. 456 — _____

7. 749 — _____

8. 4,326 — _____

Round the numbers on these marshmallows to the nearest 1,000.

9. 4,754 — 5,000

10. 3,357 — _____

11. 8,267 — _____

12. 9,701 — _____

ON YOUR OWN

Build a model campsite using miniature marshmallows and toothpicks. Stick the toothpicks into the marshmallows to make tent and cabin shapes.

The **main idea** of a story is what the story is mostly about.
Read the paragraph below, then answer questions about the main idea.

The Landers family couldn't wait to go camping. Four days in the fresh mountain air were just what they needed. Kurt planned on hiking to Mirror Lake. Amelia hoped to go on a horseback ride. Mr. Landers wanted to go bird watching. Mrs. Landers brought her sketch pad so that she could draw pictures of the delicate meadow flowers. It was going to be a vacation that the whole family would enjoy.

What is the main idea of the paragraph?

_____

_____

_____

Read each group of ideas. Then write a main idea for each group.

build a campfire	tell stories
toast marshmallows	look at the stars

The main idea is:

_____

_____

FAST FACT

Arches National Park in Arizona has more than 2,000 rock arches that were created by erosion. The largest is called Landscape Arch and is 306 feet long. There is a campground 18 miles from the park's entrance.

packing a suitcase	making campground reservations
checking a road map	illing up the car's gas tank

The main idea is:

_____

_____

mountain biking	hiking
swimming	horseback riding

The main idea is:

_____

_____

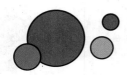
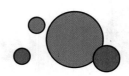

CAMP CURSIVE

Trace the cursive letters.

Aa   Bb   Cc   Dd

Ee   Ff   Gg   Hh

Ii   Jj   Kk   Ll

Mm   Nn   Oo   Pp

Qq   Rr   Ss   Tt

Uu   Vv   Ww   Xx

Yy   Zz

ON YOUR OWN
Practice writing your first, middle, and last name in cursive letters.

CREATIVE CONSTELLATIONS

Constellations are groups of stars that together form a picture in the sky.
Here are some star maps that show three constellations that can be seen in the summer months.

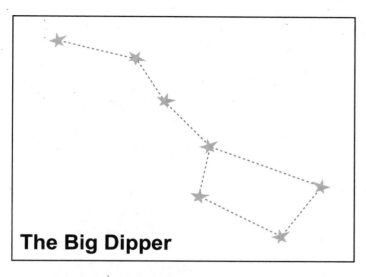

The Big Dipper

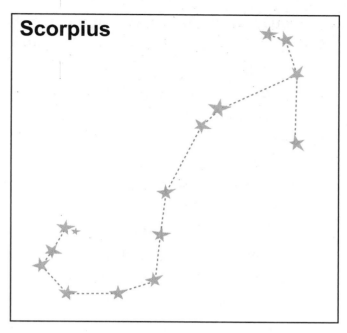

Scorpius

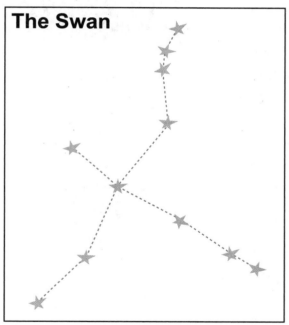

The Swan

How do you think these constellations got their names?

_____

_____

_____

_____

_____

_____

FUN FACT

The Big Dipper is one of the easiest constellations to find in the sky. Two of the stars in the Big Dipper always point to the north.

HOME, SWEET HOME

Read the story. Then answer the questions.

Before the Europeans came to North America, there were five main cultural groups of Native Americans. Each group had its own way of life and lived in its own type of home. Native Americans used the natural resources around them to build their homes.

The Northwest Indians lived in wooden lodges. Each lodge was large enough for several families to live together. The lodges were built from wood and bark. Outside of each lodge, there was a totem pole.

The California-Intermountain Indians lived in wickiups. These were circular homes made from arched poles and covered with brush.

The Southwest Indians lived in pueblos. Pueblos were apartment-style buildings made from adobe and clay. Many families lived together in each apartment and new rooms were added as the families grew.

The Plains Indians used buffalo skins to make tepees. The skins were attached to long wooden poles and decorated with paints. Tepees could be put up and taken down quickly so that the people could follow the buffalo.

The Eastern Woodland Indians lived in longhouses. These homes were similar to the Northwest Indian homes. They were built from wooden frames and covered in bark. Several families lived together in each home.

1. Why did Native Americans live in different kinds of homes? _____

_____

2. Which two groups lived in homes that were similar to each other? What kind of environment do you think these groups lived in? _____

_____

3. Which group of Native Americans probably moved around the most? How would their type of homes help them to do this? _____

_____

FACES IN THE MOUNTAIN

Mount Rushmore is in the Black Hills of South Dakota. It is a monument to honor George Washington, Thomas Jefferson, Theodore Roosevelt, and Abraham Lincoln. These men were American presidents.

If you were hired to design a sculpture that would honor four American heroes, who would you choose to feature in your sculpture? Draw a picture of your design here.

Write about why you selected these people for your sculpture.

_____

_____

_____

_____

_____

FAST FACT

Just 17 miles away from Mount Rushmore, another mountain sculpture is being created. It is of the great Indian leader Crazy Horse. The sculpture was started in 1948, and work on it still continues today. When it is completed, it will be the largest mountain sculpture in the world.

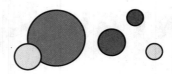

BEACH BALL BONANZA

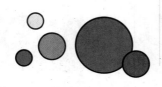

Multiply the numbers in the beach balls.

1. 2 x 6 =

_12_

2. 3 x 8 =

_____

3. 5 x 5 =

_____

4. 9 x 2 =

_____

5. 4 x 1 =

_____

6. 8 x 5 =

_____

7. 6 x 7 =

_____

8. 5 x 2 =

_____

9. 3 x 7 =

_____

ON YOUR OWN

Roll two dice and multiply the numbers together. Keep track of how many rolls it takes for you to solve all of the 36 problems that are possible.

10. 4 x 4 =

_____

11. 8 x 1 =

_____

12. 5 x 9 =

_____

SHARING SHELLS

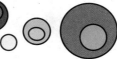

Circle the shells to solve the problems.
Write the answers.

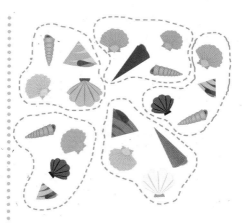

1. 20 ÷ 4 = __5__

2. 12 ÷ 3 = _____

3. 18 ÷ 6 = _____

Solve the problems.

4. 20 ÷ 5 = _____

5. 15 ÷ 3 = _____

6. 10 ÷ 2 = _____

7. 40 ÷ 4 = _____

8. 9 ÷ 3 = _____

9. 12 ÷ 4 = _____

10. 16 ÷ 4 = _____

11. 25 ÷ 5 = _____

12. 18 ÷ 6 = _____

ON YOUR OWN

Collect a variety of shells to use for decoration. You can glue some shells onto a comb handle, on a lampshade, or on gift-wrapped packages. You could also fill a vase with shells and water for a pretty table decoration.

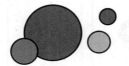 # IN OTHER WORDS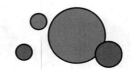

A **thesaurus** gives synonyms for words.
Sometimes it also gives antonyms.

Look at the entries below. Underline the synonyms. Circle the antonyms.

1. happy <u>glad</u>, <u>cheerful</u>, (sad,) (gloomy,) <u>joyous</u>, (unhappy,) <u>joyful</u>, <u>merry</u>

2. hot chilly, cold, fiery, frosty, flaming, scorching, frozen, sweaty

3. sparkling glistening, dark, glittery, glimmering, dim, gloomy, shimmering, murky

happy	glad	cheerful	sad	gloomy
joyous	unhappy	joyful		merry
hot	fiery	flaming	scorching	sweaty
chilly	cold	frosty	frozen	
sparkling	glistening	glittery		glimmering
shimmering	dark	dim	gloomy	murky

Choose synonyms from the box to rewrite these sentences.

4. It was a hot day at the beach. I went for a swim in the sparkling water.

_____

_____

5. Choose antonyms to rewrite the sentences again.

_____

_____

A thesaurus is organized like a dictionary. It lists words alphabetically. Guide words at the top of the page tell the first and the last words on each page.

Read the sets of guide words. Circle the words that would go on the same page.

6. beach/beneath before, beyond, blast

7. cloudy/comment common, cold, clean

8. ocean/open odor, operate, ornament

THE ENDINGS

A **suffix** is a small group of letters added to the end of a word.
A suffix changes the meaning of the word.

Suffix	Meaning	Example
-er and *-or*	*one who_____ .*	*farm + er = farmer*
-ful	*full of _____ .*	*thought + ful = thoughtful*
-less	*without _____ .*	*care + less = careless*

Rewrite each sentence. Change the underlined words to words that have the suffixes of **-er**, **-or**, **-ful**, or **-less**.

1. The <u>person swimming</u> caught the lifeguard's attention.

    The swimmer caught the lifeguard's attention.

2. He was <u>without a thought</u> and had drifted out to deep water.

    _____

3. A <u>man sailing</u> was <u>full of care</u> when he tossed the life jacket.

    _____

4. "I am <u>full of thanks</u> that you rescued me," he said.

    _____

5. The lifeguard told him that he should hire a <u>person who teaches swimming</u>.

    _____

6. "You have been so <u>full of help</u>," said the swimmer.

    _____

ON YOUR OWN

Make a crossword puzzle with words that
end in **-er**, **-or**, **-ful**, and **-less**. Write clues for
your puzzle and give it to a friend to solve.

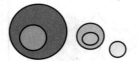

MIXED-UP PICNIC

There's a picnic at the beach, but things have gotten all mixed up!
Help fix the picnic by writing instructions for making a sandwich. Use all the words in the word box.

first	**second**	**then**
next	**last**	

_____

_____

_____

_____

_____

_____

ON YOUR OWN

Work with some friends to write "instruction puzzles." Have each person write down, in the correct order, the steps needed to complete a certain task. Cut the steps apart so that each one is on a different strip of paper. Mix up the strips and see if you and your friends can put them back together again in the correct order.

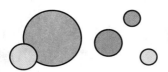

RIDE THE WAVES

Read the story. Then answer the questions.

The seashore is where the ocean meets the land. At high tide, ocean water covers much of the land at the shore. At low tide, the water rolls back into the ocean and we see the sloping shore. Tides change from day to day throughout the month. They are created by the force of gravity between the Moon, Earth, and the Sun. When the Moon, Earth, and the Sun are in line with each other, there will be spring tides. Spring tides come in very high and then go back out to sea very far. They occur every 14 to 15 days, during a new moon or a full moon. When the Moon, Earth, and the Sun are at right angles to each other, neap tides occur. During neap tides, there is little difference between the heights of high tide and low tide. Neap tides form during the first and last quarters of the Moon's cycle.

1. What happens to the shore during high tide?

Ocean water covers much of the land at the shore.

2. What creates the tides?

_____

3. Why are the tides different from day to day?

_____

4. What are spring tides? When do they occur?

_____

5. During neap tides, how are the Moon, Earth, and the Sun aligned with each other?

_____

_____

ON YOUR OWN

Study the Moon during the month. On each day of a calendar, draw a small picture of how the Moon looked on that evening. At the end of the month, look back over the calendar. Do you see any patterns in the phases of the Moon?

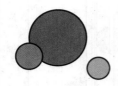
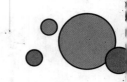

OCEAN PREDATORS

Read the story. Then solve the puzzle.

When people think of **predators**, they often think of large, fierce animals that hunt and capture other animals. While this is accurate, a predator is any animal that kills its own food. The animals that are hunted and killed are called **prey**. In the ocean, there are strong, massive predators that swim in the open water, as well as smaller predators that bury themselves in the sand or hide in caves. Ocean predators use many different methods to hunt. Elephant seals, great white sharks, and barracudas use their speed and strength to overpower other animals. Others, like stonefish and spotted groupers, use camouflage to hide themselves until their prey swims close enough to be captured. An anglerfish lures its prey with a long, thin fin that glows and wiggles. Once a fish is attracted to the lure, the anglerfish opens its mouth and sucks in its victim. Some ocean animals, like killer whales and bluefish, hunt in groups. Working together, these predators confuse their prey, cut off their escape routes, and often drive them to exhaustion. A predator's senses are perhaps its most important set of hunting tools. Without the ability to locate food, using sight, sound, or smell, the predator would have little ability to feed itself.

Down

1. Stonefish method for capturing prey
2. Hunted animals
4. Anglerfish uses its fin as this

Across

2. Hunter
3. Type of fish that hunts in groups
5. Type of fish that uses speed and strength to hunt
6. Important hunting tools

FAST FACT

A shark never has to worry about losing a tooth. The front teeth have rows and rows of replacement teeth behind them. If a tooth is lost or broken, a new tooth will grow in quickly.

AROUND THE WORLD

Color the world map. Label the oceans and the continents.

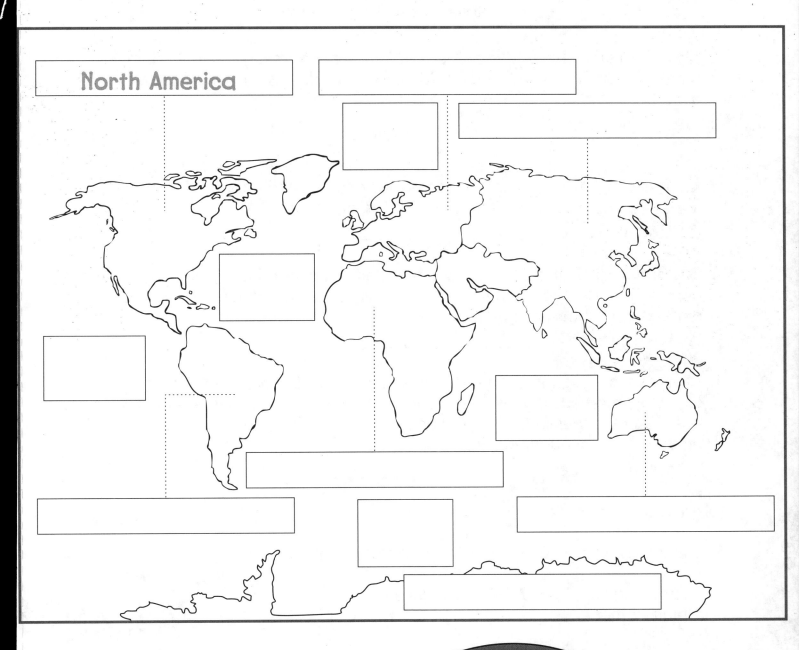

North America

PLACE VALUE IN THE PARK

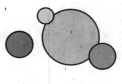

Read each puzzle. Write the number.

1. My ones digit is 3. My tens digit is 2 less than my ones digit. My hundreds digit is 3 times larger than my tens digit. My thousands digit is 1 more than my hundreds digit.

   What's my number? _____4,313_____

2. My ones digit is 3. My tens digit is 4 more than my ones digit. My hundreds digit is 2 less than my tens digit. My thousands digit is 1 more than my hundreds digit. My ten-thousands digit is half of my thousands digit.

   What's my number? _____

3. My hundreds digit is 2. My tens digit is half of my hundreds digit. My thousands digit is 4 times larger than my tens digit. My ones digit is double my thousands digit. My ten-thousands digit is 6 more than my hundreds digit.

   What's my number? _____

4. My thousands digit is 4. My ten-thousands digit is 5 more than my thousands digit. My hundreds digit is 2 less than my thousands digit. My tens digit is 4 less than my thousands digit. My ones digit is less than my thousands digit, but greater than my hundreds digit.

   What's my number? _____

Follow each set of directions.

5. Use the digits **6, 9, 0, 2**. Write the smallest 4-digit number. _____

6. Use the digits **1, 3, 5, 7**. Write the greatest 4-digit number. _____

ON YOUR OWN
Separate out the number cards from a deck of playing cards. Shuffle the cards and draw four at a time. Use these four cards to make the largest number possible. Then make the smallest number using the same cards. Continue playing until all of the cards have been drawn.

Unit cost is the price of a single item.
To find the unit cost, divide the total price by the number of items.
Determine the unit cost for each item below.

| **Plastic Forks**
8 per box
$3.20 | **Paper Plates**
bag of 50
$5.00 | **Sodas**
6-pack
$3.60 | **Juice Boxes**
12 pack
$4.80 |
| **Fried Chicken**
10-piece bucket
$3.20 | **Dinner Rolls**
15 count
$4.50 | **Oranges**
8 per bag
$3.60 | **Cupcakes**
box of 12
$4.80 |

1.

The cost of 8 forks
is $3.20.

$$8\overline{)3.20} \quad .40$$

The cost of one
fork is $0.40.

2.

3.

4.

5.

6.

7.

8.

ON YOUR OWN

Look through grocery ads in your
newspaper. Make a shopping list
from the things you see in the ads.
Determine the unit cost for each
item you want to buy.

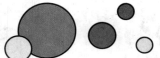 # YUM! YUM!

Help the bear find its way to the picnic basket.
Add or subtract the fractions. Put each fraction in the lowest terms.
Then color the boxes that have answers with odd numerators.

$\frac{5}{8} + \frac{2}{8} = \frac{7}{8}$	$\frac{1}{4} + \frac{2}{4} =$	$\frac{2}{6} + \frac{2}{6} =$

$\frac{8}{12} + \frac{2}{12} =$	$\frac{3}{16} - \frac{1}{16} =$	$\frac{3}{5} + \frac{1}{5} =$	$\frac{7}{10} + \frac{2}{10} =$	$\frac{11}{12} + \frac{3}{12} =$
$\frac{7}{8} - \frac{1}{8} =$	$\frac{1}{4} + \frac{2}{4} =$	$\frac{3}{8} + \frac{4}{8} =$	$\frac{8}{10} - \frac{1}{10} =$	$\frac{6}{7} - \frac{2}{7} =$
$\frac{8}{12} - \frac{2}{12} =$	$\frac{2}{6} + \frac{3}{6} =$	$\frac{10}{10} - \frac{2}{10} =$	$\frac{5}{6} - \frac{3}{6} =$	$\frac{1}{4} + \frac{3}{4} =$
$\frac{1}{3} + \frac{1}{3} =$	$\frac{5}{9} + \frac{2}{9} =$	$\frac{4}{8} - \frac{1}{8} =$	$\frac{7}{11} - \frac{3}{11} =$	$\frac{8}{9} - \frac{4}{9} =$
$\frac{3}{12} + \frac{3}{12} =$	$\frac{4}{11} - \frac{2}{11} =$	$\frac{1}{5} + \frac{2}{5} =$		

SOUND-ALIKES

Homophones are words that sound alike, but they are spelled differently and have different meanings.

Use the pairs of homophones to complete the sentences.

bare / bear	**fir / fur**	**close / clothes**
chews / choose	**ate / eight**	**creek / creak**

1. Elena dipped her __bare__ feet into the cool __creek__.

2. Which _____ would you _____ to wear?

3. The _____ scratched at its _____.

4. We _____ near the _____ tree.

5. When I _____ the lid to the picnic basket, I hear it _____.

6. My terrier _____ on _____ bones a day.

Homographs are words that look and sound alike but have different meanings.
Each word below has more than one meaning. Draw a picture to show two of the word's meanings.

7. bat

8. bill

9. palm

ON YOUR OWN
Make a list of as many homophone pairs as you can. Use each word in a sentence.

73

PERSONALITY PLUS

Authors use descriptions, dialogue, and actions to make their characters come to life.
Read the passages below. Write a description of each character's personality based on what you read.

1. The blistering sun seared Moira's skin. She dabbed at her forehead with the edge of her shirt sleeve. She looked toward the top of the hill and took a gulp of water. "I'm almost there," she said to herself. "I'm not giving up until I make it."

_____

_____

2. Daniel raced through the park. He couldn't believe he was late again. He hoped his coach wouldn't bench him. Today's game was for the championship and Daniel just had to play. Suddenly, he stopped dead in his tracks. "Holy cow!" he said. "I left my bat at home."

_____

_____

3. Alicia peeked into the box of cookies. She counted two, four, six, eight. "There's enough for two each," she told her brother and sister. When they weren't looking, Alicia slipped the extra two cookies into her pocket.

_____

_____

4. Noah looked through his binoculars and found the robin's nest. The eggs had finally hatched and he could hear the tiny birds inside. He looked around for the parent birds but did not see them anywhere. "Don't worry," he whispered to the babies. "I'll make sure you're safe until they get back."

_____

_____

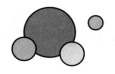 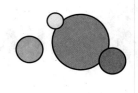

Plants, like animals, can reproduce. This means that plants can make new plants like themselves. Different plants reproduce in different ways. Flowering plants use pollen to reproduce. The pollen is transferred from one flower to another, either by wind or by insects. Large amounts of pollen are produced to make sure that some will be caught by other flowers. Many plants reproduce by growing buds that drop off the plant and start new lives of their own. Other plants make spores that are carried away by wind or rain. When the spores land in a suitable place, they grow into new plants.

Look at the pictures below. Write a sentence for each one that describes how the plant most likely reproduces.

1. _____
_____
_____
_____

2. _____
_____
_____
_____

3. _____
_____
_____
_____

ON YOUR OWN
Gather some dandelions and blow the seeds off the flowers. Watch as the seeds spin through the air. Then write a paragraph about what you think happened to the seeds.

SUMMER CELEBRATIONS

People all around the world participate in special celebrations during the summer.

Each August, the Buddhist festival of Esala Perahera is held in Kandy, Sri Lanka. Elephants, dancers, acrobats, and drummers parade through the streets. The festival lasts for 10 nights, with the festivities of each night becoming grander than the night before.

Another August festival is the Raksha Bandhan. This is a Hindu celebration that takes place in India. During the festival, brothers and sisters celebrate their love for one another. Sisters give their brothers bracelets to wear and brothers vow to protect their sisters.

Many countries celebrate their independence days during the summer. The United States, Canada, Argentina, and Belgium are just a few.

Plan a summer celebration of your own. What would your celebration be for? What kinds of things would you do at your celebration? Draw a picture to show something from your celebration. Write a few sentences about it.

MAKE A DIFFERENCE

Good citizens follow rules and obey laws. They work to help make their communities better. They take good care of our planet Earth. List some of the things that good citizens in your community do.

Follow rules and obey laws

_____
_____
_____
_____
_____
_____
_____
_____

Take care of our planet Earth

_____
_____
_____
_____
_____
_____
_____
_____

Make communities better

_____
_____
_____
_____
_____
_____
_____

ON YOUR OWN

Do some investigating about the needs in your community. Then plan a service project to help meet one of the needs. Invite some of your friends to join you, and see the difference you can all make!

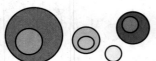 # FUN AT THE FAIR

Perimeter is the distance around a shape.
To find a shape's perimeter, add the length of its sides.

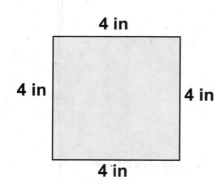

4 in
4 in   **4 in**
4 in

4 + 4 + 4 + 4 = 16 inches
This square has a perimeter of 16 inches.

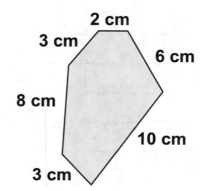

2 cm
3 cm
6 cm
8 cm
10 cm
3 cm

2 + 6 + 10 + 3 + 8 + 3 = 32 centimeters
This polygon has a perimeter of 32 centimeters.

Find the perimeter of each animal pen at the county fair.

1. _____

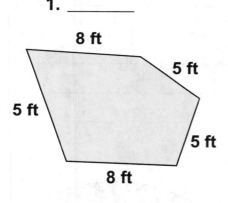

8 ft
5 ft
5 ft
5 ft
8 ft

2. _____

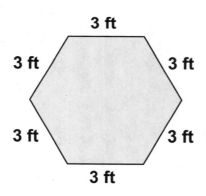

3 ft
3 ft   **3 ft**
3 ft   **3 ft**
3 ft

3. _____

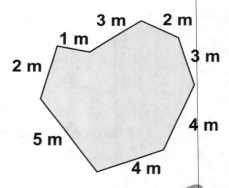

3 m   **2 m**
1 m
2 m   **3 m**
5 m   **4 m**
4 m

4. _____

5 ft
5 ft   **5 ft**
5 ft   **5 ft**
5 ft   **5 ft**
5 ft   **5 ft**
5 ft   **5 ft**
5 ft

5. _____

6 m   **6 m**
10 m

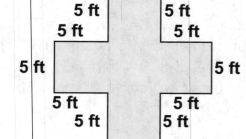

ON YOUR OWN

Use a measuring tape to find the perimeter of each room in your home. Which room has the largest perimeter? Which has the smallest?

QUILTING BEE

The county fair has a quilt exhibit.
Name the shape of each piece found in the quilts. Use the words in the word box to help you.

1.

hexagon

2.

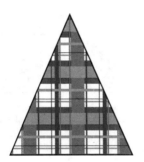

_____

3.

_____

4.

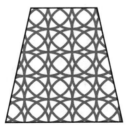

_____

5.

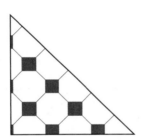

_____

6.

_____

7.

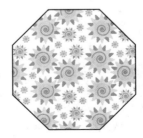

_____

8.

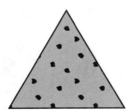

_____

FAST FACT

Many people think of quilting as an American invention, but quilting has been around for thousands of years. In Ancient Egypt, quilting was used mostly for clothing and there is some evidence that kings and queens wore quilted garments.

TELL ME ABOUT IT

Authors try to make their writing as interesting as possible.
One way to do this is to describe sights, sounds, tastes, smells, and textures in detail.
Write your own descriptions of the following experiences. Use as much detail as possible.

Eating cotton candy

_____
_____
_____
_____

Riding a Ferris wheel

_____
_____
_____
_____

Visiting a petting zoo

_____
_____
_____
_____

Watching a fireworks show

_____
_____
_____
_____

FAST FACT

Can you guess what cotton candy is made of? It's pure sugar! The machine used to make cotton candy melts the sugar, then spins the liquid around. The liquid sugar is pushed through holes in the machine and when it hits the air, it cools and becomes a solid again.

STICK TO THE TOPIC

A **paragraph** is a group of sentences that all tell about one thing.
The **topic sentence** tells what the paragraph is about.
The other sentences give details about the main topic.
Read the topic sentence in the middle of the web.
Complete the web by writing sentences that support the topic sentence.

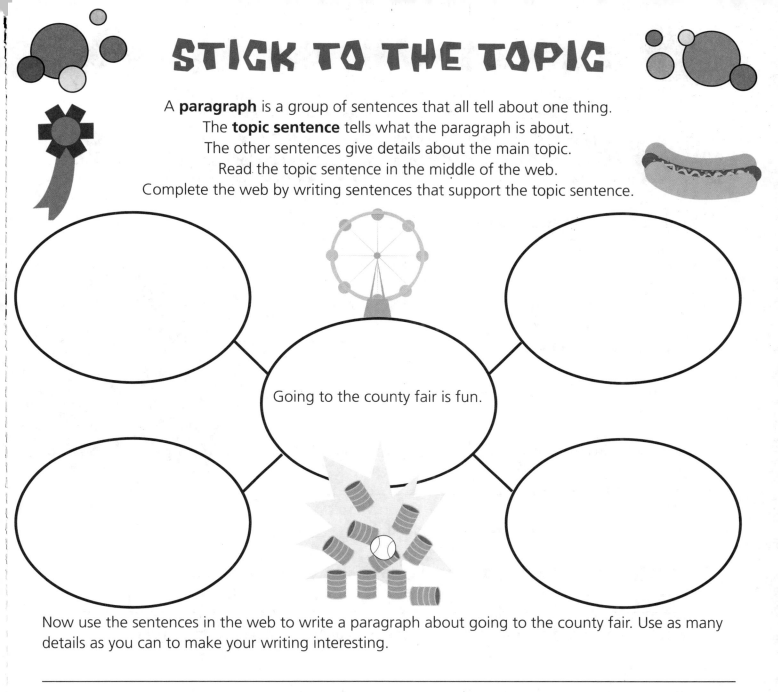

Going to the county fair is fun.

Now use the sentences in the web to write a paragraph about going to the county fair. Use as many details as you can to make your writing interesting.

_____

_____

_____

_____

_____

_____

ON YOUR OWN
Create a family newsletter to share stories about your hobbies, your vacations, and your favorite things. Ask each member of your family to contribute an article for the newsletter. When it's complete, mail it to family members.

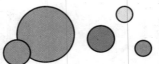

LOOK IT UP

Which type of reference material would you use for the following information?
Choose from the materials listed in the word box.

dictionary	thesaurus	atlas	encyclopedia	almanac

1. the meaning of the word **heifer** ___dictionary___

2. the number of people who work on farms in your state _____

3. the history of the Ferris wheel _____

4. another word for **fair** _____

5. a map of your state _____

Answer the questions below by using the references at the top of the page.

6. What does **heifer** mean? _____

7. How many people in your state work on farms? _____

8. What is one interesting fact about the history of the Ferris wheel? _____

_____

9. What is another word for fair that has a similar meaning to "a gathering for people"?

_____

10. What are the names of some of the towns and cities around your community?

_____

ON YOUR OWN
Choose a topic that you are interested in. Do some research on your topic to learn more about it. See how many different types of reference materials you can use in your research.

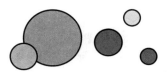
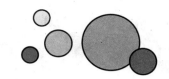

BRAIN POWER

Look at this diagram of the human brain.

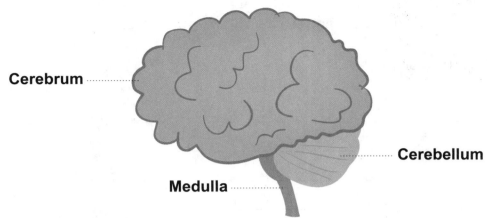

Cerebrum

Cerebellum

Medulla

medulla controls involuntary movements such as your heartbeat

cerebellum controls voluntary movements like walking

cerebrum allows you to think, make decisions, remember, and imagine

Draw a line to the part of the brain that you use for each of the following activities.

1. breathing

2. running

3. lifting your arm

4. memorizing math facts

5. blinking

6. writing a story

7. choosing what clothes to wear

8. throwing a baseball

Medulla

Cerebellum

Cerebrum

FAST FACT
It is thought that each side of the brain controls different things. The left side controls your speech and language skills. The right side controls your emotions and creativity.

 # YOUR FAMILY

Your **ancestors** are members of your family who lived a long time ago. Find out more about your ancestors by interviewing a parent or grandparent. Ask where your ancestors came from. Ask to hear a story about and see a picture of your ancestors.

Write a paragraph about your ancestors.

_____

_____

_____

_____

_____

_____

_____

Draw a picture of your ancestors.

TRIVIA TIME

Match the names of the heroes with their accomplishments.
Use reference material if you need help.

Thomas Jefferson

Harriet Tubman

Laura Ingalls Wilder

Abraham Lincoln

Frederick Douglass

Benjamin Franklin

Susan B. Anthony

Martin Luther King, Jr.

Leader of the Women's Rights Movement

Used the Underground Railroad to help slaves escape

16th president; wrote the Emancipation Proclamation to end slavery

Leader of the Civil Rights Movement

3rd president; wrote the Declaration of Independence

Author and editor who spoke out against slavery

Inventor and patriot who helped with the American Revolution

Author of children's books about pioneer life.

FAST FACT

Benjamin Franklin lived from 1706 to 1790. In addition to being one of America's Founding Fathers, he was also a painter, scientist, inventor, musician, printer, philosopher, and economist!

Dana has 3 red shirts, 3 blue shirts, 2 green shirts, and 1 yellow shirt.
Dana has decided to play a game to decide which color to wear.
Follow the instructions to play Dana's game.

- Cut 3 red squares, 3 blue squares, 2 green squares, and 1 yellow square from colored paper.
- Place the squares in a paper bag.
- Draw one square at a time. Record the color on the graph and then put the square back into the bag.
- Repeat until you have drawn 50 squares.
- The color that is drawn the most is the color that Dana will wear to school.

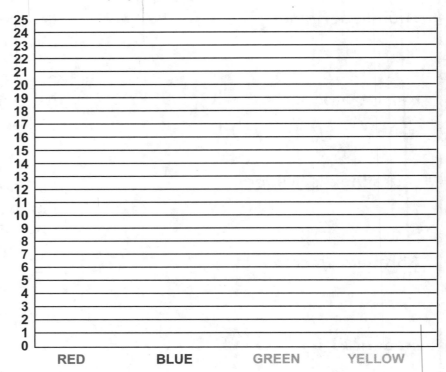

RED   BLUE   GREEN   YELLOW

1. Which color was chosen the most? _____

2. Which color was chosen the least? _____

3. Which two colors had an equal chance of being chosen? _____

ON YOUR OWN
Which clothes will you wear on the first day of school? Play a game like Dana's to help you decide.

SCHOOL SUPPLIES

Marcus is going shopping for school supplies.
He has $40.00 to spend. Look at the school supplies below, then answer the questions.

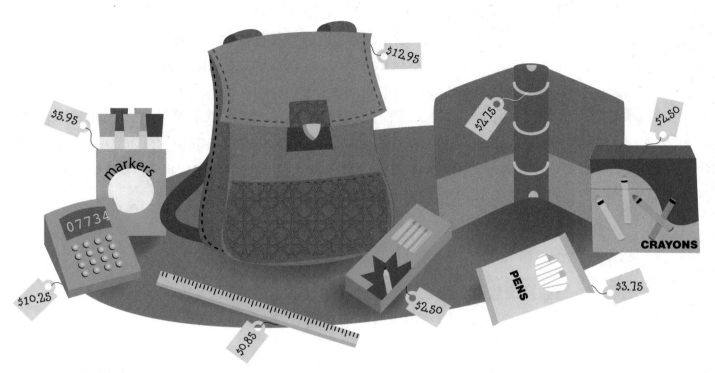

1. Marcus bought a backpack, a binder, and pens. How much did he spend?

   $12.95 + $ 2.75 + $ 3.75 = $19.45

   How much does he have left over? $40.00 − $19.45 = $20.55

2. Marcus bought crayons, a ruler, and a calculator. How much did he spend?

   _____

   How much does he have left over? _____

3. Marcus bought pencils, markers, and a binder. How much did he spend?

   _____

   How much does he have left over? _____

4. Marcus bought a binder, markers, and a ruler. How much did he spend?

   _____

   How much does he have left over? _____

5. Marcus bought a calculator, pens, and crayons. How much did he spend?

   _____

   How much does he have left over? _____

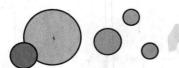 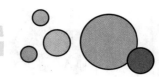
Read the story. Then answer the questions.

The sun shines through Tina's window and she wakes with a smile. Today is going to be a great day! Tina goes to her closet and picks out her very best school outfit. After she gets dressed, she puts her new notebooks and pencils into her backpack. Her dad serves pancakes and eggs for breakfast while her mom packs her lunch. Then her mom drives her to the first day of school. Tina sees her friend, Becca, in front of the school office. "Great news!" says Becca. "We're in the same class again!" The girls drop their backpacks near the classroom door and head out to the playground. Tina can't wait for the bell to ring. Third grade is going to be fantastic!

1. Why do you think Tina wakes up with a smile?

_____

2. What does Tina do to get ready for school?

_____

3. What is special about this day?

_____

4. Who is Becca?

_____

5. What is Becca's good news?

_____

6. What grade is Tina in?

_____

ON YOUR OWN
Write a short story about a child's first day at school. Think about how the character in your story might feel. Is he or she excited or nervous? Does the character expect to have good experiences or bad ones? Choose words and images that will help tell about the character's mood.

MY SUMMER VACATION

Think about some of the different things you did this summer. Write some of the things in the clouds. Choose one idea and write a paragraph about it on the schoolhouse.

THE REASON FOR THE SEASONS

Read the story. Then answer the questions.

In most parts of the world the weather changes based on the seasons. Summer temperatures are the hottest and winter temperatures are the coldest. Spring and autumn temperatures are somewhere in-between. These changes in temperature repeat themselves year after year. Some people mistakenly believe that these temperature changes have to do with how close Earth is to the Sun during different times of the year. Actually, the seasons occur because of the angle at which the Sun's rays hit Earth. During part of the year, the northern part of Earth leans more directly toward the Sun than the southern part of Earth. This means that it is summer in the north and winter in the south. Later, the position of Earth reverses and the southern part has summer while the northern part has winter.

Circle the statements that are **true**. Cross out the statements that are **false**.

1. When it is summer in the northern part of Earth, it is winter in the southern part.

2. Winter is the warmest season.

3. Changes in temperature are completely unpredictable.

4. The seasons change because of the angles at which the Sun's rays hit Earth.

5. Summer is the warmest season.

6. Temperatures change during the year based on how close Earth is to the Sun.

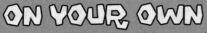

ON YOUR OWN

What is your favorite holiday? Make a poster to show how the weather affects the way you celebrate it. On the back of your poster, show how people on the opposite side of the world would celebrate the same holiday.

WHERE IN THE WORLD?

Have you ever wondered where the things that you buy come from? Some things may come from your local area. Others may come from other areas around the United States or from other countries. Most items have a label that tells where the item came from.

Collect the items below. Look at the packaging and the labels on the items to see if you can find out where they came from.

1. Your favorite book _____

2. Your favorite shirt _____

3. Your favorite shoes _____

4. Your favorite music CD _____

5. A new package of pencils _____

6. A new package of pens _____

7. A backpack _____

8. A notebook _____

ON YOUR OWN

Use a world map to find each of the places that you listed above. Mark each place to show where some of your things come from.

SUMMER READING LIST

Here are some books for readers going into third grade to enjoy during the summer months.

Freckle Juice by Judy Blume
Andrew wants freckles so badly that he spends time in class counting the freckles on his friend's neck, wishing that he, too, had freckles. When Sharon offers him a recipe for freckle juice for fifty cents, Andrew accepts. But is the recipe all that he hoped for?

Nasty, Stinky Sneakers by Eve Bunting
Colin has worked hard to win the Stinkiest Sneakers in the World contest, but just before the competition, his stinky sneakers end up missing. Can he find them in time and still win the contest?

Ramona Quimby, Age 8 by Beverly Cleary
Ramona has a new school, a new teacher, and lots of new responsibilities while her mother works and her father goes to school. All the changes she is faced with are exciting, yet difficult at the same time.

Pleasing the Ghost by Sharon Creech
Ever since Dennis's dad died, Dennis has seen a parade of ghosts coming through his bedroom. When the ghost of Uncle Arvie shows up, Dennis isn't surprised, but he has to find out what the ghost of Uncle Arvie wants.

A Jar of Tiny Stars edited by Bernice Cullinan
This collection of poems, by 10 different poets, was chosen by children. The topics range from a sleeping cat to the construction of a skyscraper, and everything in-between.

Sable by Karen Hesse
Tate is thrilled when a scruffy mutt wanders into her yard. She convinces her parents to let her keep the dog. When Tate's attempts to train Sable fail, her parents say the dog has to go.

How I Became a Pirate by Melinda Long
Jeremy Jacob joins a group of pirates for a wild seafaring adventure. He quickly learns to love the rowdiness of the pirates' lifestyle, but soon realizes that he misses having someone to tuck him in at night and provide comfort through a storm.

Tippy Lemmey by Patricia C. McKissack
Leandra and her friends are afraid of the new neighborhood dog named Tippy Lemmey. But when thieves try to steal Tippy and other neighborhood dogs, the friends come to the rescue.

Twig by Elizabeth Orton Jones
A young girl brightens up her dreary world when she invents a home for fairies from an old discarded tomato can.

The Best School Year Ever by Barbara Robinson
When a school assignment forces the sixth grade class of Woodrow Wilson Elementary School to come up with a list of compliments for each classmate, the kids learn that even bad kids like the mischievous Herdman clan have good qualities.

Sideways Stories from Wayside School
by Louis Sachar
When Wayside School was built, a terrible mistake was made. The classrooms were built one on top of the other, 30 stories high, instead of side by side. And that's just the beginning of the strange things that happen at this wacky school.

SUMMER ACTIVITIES AND PROJECTS

Art Party

Invite a group of friends over for an art party. Have a collection of various art supplies on hand such as colored paper, paints, glitter, markers, and scrap materials. See what kind of artistic masterpieces are created.

Book Club

Start a neighborhood book club. Invite each club member to select a book for the group to read. Then plan a book party for each selection. Serve snacks and talk about what you liked, or didn't like, about the story.

Bowling for Dollars

Raise money for a special charity in your community. Ask your friends and neighbors to help you throw a "bowl-a-thon" as a fundraiser. Collect pledges from people who want to help, and then donate all of the money to the charity.

Family History

Ask different members of your family if you can interview them about their lives. Take notes or record the interviews. Use the information you learn to write stories about the lives of your relatives.

Nature Watch

Choose a certain time each day to go outside and observe the plants and animals around your home. Keep a notebook where you write brief descriptions and draw sketches of what you see.

Pen Pals

Choose a friend or a relative as a summertime pen pal. Write letters back and forth to each other to describe the things that you do and the places that you visit.

Secret Code

Develop a secret code. Give your friends the key to your code, and use it to write secret messages to one another.

Sports Fest

Plan a day of sports activities for your friends. Have competitions to see who can shoot the most baskets, throw a ball the farthest, run the longest, and jump the highest. Give a small prize to the winner of each contest.

Summer Scrapbook

Use a photo album to collect mementos from your summer adventures. Place photographs, ticket stubs, letters, and postcards in the scrapbook. Write short journal entries next to the items to describe what happened.

Page 6
2. 54
3. 143
4. 100
5. 117
6. 165
7. 353
8. 804
9. 781
10. 905
11. 978
12. 600

Page 7

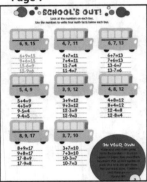

Page 8

Page 9
These are the corrected words:
turn
black
easy
skirt
square

Page 10
These are the circled sentences:
4. Everyone will dance.
6. We will serve burgers and chips.
7. We hope you can come.
Answers to questions 9 and 10 will vary.

Page 11
Singular nouns:
garden

dirt
scarecrow
kitchen
dad
salad
Plural nouns:
peppers
seeds
weeds
plants
birds
vegetables

Page 12
scissors
metal measuring spoon
metal paper clip
belt buckle

Page 13
_2_ The fabric is sent to a factory.
_6_ The customer wraps the shirt and gives it to Dad on Father's Day.
_4_ The shirt is sold to a store.
_3_ Workers at the factory cut and sew the fabric to make the shirt.
_1_ Cotton is grown, harvested, and turned into fabric.
_5_ The store sells the shirt to a customer.

Page 14
2.
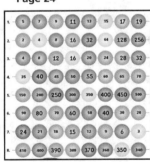
New York

3.
Seattle

4.
Chicago

5.
New Orleans

6.
Los Angeles

Page 15
These bills and coins are circled:
2. three dollar bills, two

dimes, one nickel
3. two dimes, two nickels
4. one five-dollar bill, one dollar bill, one quarter, two dimes, five pennies
5. six quarters, two dimes, one nickel
6. one five-dollar bill, three dollar bills, three quarters, two dimes
7. three dollar bills, two nickels, five pennies
8. four dollar bills, one quarter, four pennies

Page 16
Answers will vary.

Page 17
2. The directions to the lake were unclear.
3. Then Dad replaced the map into his backpack.
4. Mom and Dad were unhappy about being lost on the trail.
5. "We should have preplanned our hike," said Mom.
6. "You're right," said Dad. "We are unprepared for this."

Page 18
2. Chapter 1
3. Page 60
4. Places to eat
5. The chapter about beaches
6. Sports
7. Page 80
8. Chapter 5

Page 19
2. The caves began forming millions of years ago.
3. The caves are made from limestone.
4. These are called stalagtites.
5. Answers will vary.

Page 20

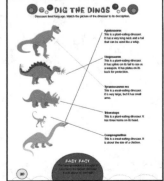

Page 21
2. Cross out "Amelia Earhart liked to sit quietly."
3. Circle "Amelia flew airplanes."
4. Cross out "Amelia drove a car across the Atlantic Ocean."
5. Circle "Amelia wanted to fly around the globe."
6. Circle "People think that Amelia's plane crashed."

Page 22
2. <
3. <
4. <
5. >
6. >
7. <
8. >
9. =
10. <
11. >
12. >

Page 23
2. 3
3. 1
4. 3
5. Cheetah Cabin
6. Bobcat Cabin, Donkey Cabin

Page 24

Page 25
2. walked
3. low
4. quiet
5. few
Answers to questions 6–11 will vary.

Page 26
Answers will vary.

Page 27
_4_ Inside the chrysalis, the caterpillar's body begins to change.
_5_ When the chrysalis opens up, a butterfly comes out.
_3_ The caterpillar hangs itself from a twig and forms a chrysalis.
_1_ A caterpillar hatches from an egg.
_2_ As the caterpillar eats and grows, it sheds its skin.

_1_ A frog egg is laid in water.
_5_ When the tail is completely gone, it has turned into a frog.
_2_ A tadpole begins to form inside the egg.
_4_ The tail starts to shrink and legs begin to grow.
_3_ The tadpole hatches from the egg with a tail and no legs.

Page 28
2. North
3. A5
4. North and East
5. Stables
6. Art Center

Page 29
2. Cowboy shirts, ties
3. hula hoop
4. sock hop
5. Dance cards

Page 30
2. 16 + 22 + 15 = 53
3. 30 x 3 = Jenna practices for 90 minutes per week.
6 hours = 360 minutes
360 ÷ 90 = 4
Jenna needs to practice for 4 weeks.
4. 12, 14, 16, 18, 20, 22, 24, 26, 29, 30
The tenth ball will go 30 feet.

Page 31
2. Game 3 and Game 6
3. 11 runs
4. 17 runs

Page 32
2. Mrs.
3. Ave.
4. Sat.
5. Wed.
6. Dr.
7. Dr.
8. Aug.

Page 33

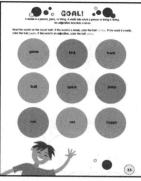

Page 34
2. Casey was excited.
3. She was nervous that she would land on her belly or crash her head on the bottom of the pool.
4. Casey was happy.
5. chuckled

Page 35
2. Cross out "It is not possible to measure the speed of a moving object."
3. Color "Kicking a soccer ball changes the position of the ball."
4. Cross out "A rolling ball can only stop if someone picks it up."
5. Cross out "The harder you kick a ball, the slower it will move."
6. Color "Friction from water slows down swimmers."

Page 36

Page 37
Answers will vary.

Page 38
2. 26 + 34 = 60; 60 − 26 = 34
3. 75 + 12 = 87; 87 − 75 = 12
4. 18 + 39 = 57; 57 − 18 = 39
5. 69 + 24 = 93; 93 − 69 = 24
6. 35 + 15 = 50; 50 − 35 = 15

7. 47 + 28 = 75; 75 − 47 = 28
8. 29 + 29 = 58; 58 − 29 = 29
9. 61 + 24 = 85; 85 − 61 = 24
10. 17 + 39 = 56; 56 − 17 = 39
11. 63 + 32 = 95; 95 − 63 = 32
12. 55 + 17 = 72; 72 − 55 = 17
BECAUSE THEY CAN'T CARRY A SUITCASE

Page 39
2. 110
3. 280
4. 159
5. 91
6. 141
7. 332
8. 390
9. 187
10. 409

Page 40
2. 108
3. 8
4. 14
5. Kiwis and Peacocks
6. b

Page 41
Sentences will be similar to these, but may vary slightly:
2. We saw lions, tigers, and bears.
3. I liked the tigers the best, but my brother liked the bears better.
4. After lunch we went to see the monkeys and the polar bears.
5. We shopped at the gift shop before we left and my brother and I bought T-shirts.
6. I was sad to leave the zoo because I wanted to stay longer.

Page 42
2. .
3. ?
4. ?
5. .
6. !
Sentences will vary.

Page 43
The White-winged Duck is a bird.
The Whooping Crane is a bird.
The Silver Shark is a fish.
The African Elephant is a mammal.
The Blue Whale is a mammal.

Page 44
2. Lions
3. Gorillas
4. You head southeast to get from the gorillas to the giraffes. Then continue east to get to the elephants.

Page 45
2. White House
3. Liberty Bell
4. "The Star-Spangled Banner"
5. flag
6. Statue of Liberty

Page 46
2. 35
3. 48
4. 27
5. 30

Page 47
2. 3
3. 9
4. 8
5. 3
6. 11

Page 48
2. barnyard
3. buttermilk
4. cornbread
5. watermelon
6. haystack
7. scarecrow
8. wheelbarrow

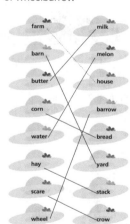

Page 49
In July, Becky and Jim visited Aunt Tonya's farm. On their first day there, they swam in Sunstone Creek. Afterward, they hiked up Butler's Hill. The next day they collected eggs! Aunt Tonya said they could sell the eggs at the farmers' market on Main Street. On Saturday, they helped clean the horse stalls before their riding lessons. That evening, Aunt

Tonya took everyone on a hayride. Becky and Jim had a great time on the farm.

Page 50
1. b
2. a
3. d
4. b
5. b

Page 51
2. leaves
3. fruit
4. roots
5. water; nutrients
6. sunlight; air
7. roots
8. seeds

Page 52
Answers will vary.

Page 53
1. c
2. a
3. a
4. c
5. a

Page 54
2. 3,540; 3,640; 3,740; 3,840; 3,940; 4,040
3. 405; 435; 465; 495; 525; 555
4. 1,425; 1,675; 1,925; 2,175; 2,425; 2,675
5. 7,000; 7,500; 8,000; 8,500; 9,000; 9,500
6. 3,372; 4,372; 5,372; 6,372; 7,372; 8,372

Page 55
2. 6,000 + 700 + 30 + 2
3. 8,000 + 300 + 80 + 8
4. 3,000 + 900 + 50 + 4
5. 2,000 + 500 + 40 + 2
6. 4,000 + 300 + 20 + 0
7. 5,000 + 500 + 50 + 5
8. 7,000 + 0 + 20 + 1

Page 56
2. 70
3. 130
4. 2,320
6. 500
7. 700
8. 4,300
10. 3,000
11. 8,000
12. 10,000

Page 57
Answers will vary.

Page 58
This page is complete when all the letters are traced.

Page 59
The constellations got their names based on how they look in the sky.

Page 60
1. Each had different natural resources with which to build their homes.
2. The Northwest Indians and Eastern Woodland Indians lived in similar homes. This is probably because they had wood to use to build their homes.
3. The Plains Indians moved around the most. They could easily take their tepees with them when they moved.

Page 61
Answers will vary.

Page 62
2. 24
3. 25
4. 18
5. 4
6. 40
7. 42
8. 10
9. 21
10. 16
11. 8
12. 45

Page 63
2. 4
3. 3
4. 4
5. 5
6. 5
7. 10
8. 3
9. 3
10. 4
11. 5
12. 3

Page 64
2. Underline these words: fiery, flaming, scorching, sweaty
Circle these words: chilly, cold, frosty, frozen
3. Underline these words: glistening, glittery, glimmering, shimmering
Circle these words: dark, dim, gloomy, murky
4. Answers will vary.
5. Answers will vary.
6. before
7. cold
8. odor

Page 65
2. He was thoughtless and had drifted out to deep water.
3. A sailor was careful when he tossed the life jacket.
4. "I am thankful that you rescued me," he said.
5. The lifeguard told him that he should hire a swimming teacher.
6. "You have been so helpful," said the swimmer.

Page 66
Answers will vary.

Page 67
2. The tides are created by the force of gravity between the Moon, Earth, and the Sun.
3. The tides are different because Earth, the Moon, and the Sun are not always at the same angle.
4. Spring tides are when the tides come in very high and then go back out to sea very far. They occur when the Moon, Earth, and the Sun are in line with each other.
5. Neap tides occur when the Moon, Earth, and the Sun are at right angles to each other.

Page 68
Down:
2. prey
4. lure

Across:
2. predator
3. bluefish
5. barracuda
6. senses

Page 69

Page 70
2. 36,573
3. 84,218
4. 94,203
5. 2,069
6. 7,531

Page 71
2. 10 cents
3. 60 cents
4. 40 cents
5. 32 cents
6. 30 cents
7. 45 cents
8. 40 cents

Page 72

Page 73
2. clothes; choose
3. bear; fur
4. ate; fir
5. close; creak
6. chews; eight
Pictures drawn will vary.

Page 74
Answers will vary.

Page 75
Answers will vary.

Page 76
Answers will vary.

Page 77
Answers will vary.

Page 78
1. 31 ft
2. 18 ft
3. 24 m
4. 60 ft
5. 22 m

Page 79
2. isosceles triangle
3. pentagon
4. trapezoid
5. right triangle
6. heptagon
7. octagon
8. equilateral triangle

Page 80
Answers will vary.

Page 81
Answers will vary.

Page 82
2. almanac
3. encyclopedia
4. thesaurus
5. atlas
6. **Heifer** is another word for cow.
7. Answers will vary
8. Answers will vary.
9. Answers will vary.
10. Answers will vary.

Page 83

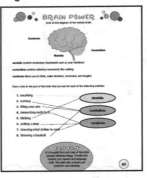

Page 84
Answers will vary.

Page 85

Page 86
Answers will vary.

Page 87
2. $13.60; $26.40
3. $11.20; $28.80
4. $9.55; $30.45
5. $16.50; $23.50

Page 88
1. Tina is excited for the first day of school.
2. Tina picks an outfit, gets notebooks and pencils, and eats breakfast to get ready for school.
3. Today is special because it is the first day of third grade.
4. Becca is Tina's friend.
5. Becca's good news is that she and Tina are in the same class.
6. Tina is in third grade.

Page 89
Answers will vary.

Page 90
2. false
3. false
4. true
5. true
6. false

Page 91
Answers will vary.